Canvas LMS Course Design

Design, build, and teach your very own online course using the powerful tools of the Canvas Learning Management System

Ryan John

BIRMINGHAM - MUMBAI

Canvas LMS Course Design

First published: August 2014

Production reference: 1180814

Published by Packt Publishing Ltd.
Livery Place
35 Livery Street
Birmingham B3 2PB, UK.

ISBN 978-1-78216-064-9

www.packtpub.com

Cover image by Shweta Suresh Karkera (shwetaimages@gmail.com)

Credits

Author
Ryan John

Reviewers
Deb Cook

Elizabeth Dennis

Travis Thurston

Donna Harp Ziegenfuss, Ed.D.

Acquisition Editor
Joanne Fitzpatrick

Content Development Editor
Priya Singh

Technical Editors
Venu Manthena

Nachiket Vartak

Copy Editors
Deepa Nambiar

Adithi Shetty

Stuti Srivastava

Project Coordinator
Swati Kumari

Proofreaders
Simran Bhogal

Ameesha Green

Paul Hindle

Indexers
Hemangini Bari

Mariammal Chettiyar

Tejal Soni

Priya Subramani

Production Coordinator
Nilesh R. Mohite

Cover Work
Nilesh R. Mohite

About the Author

Ryan John is a graduate of Westminster Choir College of Rider University, where he spent 3 years as a Technical Assistant for the pilot program of the Instructure Canvas Learning Management System at Rider University. While at Rider and Westminster, he served as a Technical Assistant, Course Designer, and Course Consultant for over a dozen courses offered by Westminster Choir College, the Westminster Office of Continuing Education, and the Westminster Center for Critical Pedagogy. During Rider's university-wide implementation of the Instructure Canvas LMS, he assisted with faculty training sessions and individual tutorials in course organization, design, and management.

In addition to his work in online course design, Ryan serves on the editorial board of *Visions of Research in Music Education*, the scholarly journal of the New Jersey Music Educators Association. He has worked as a freelance copy editor, both privately and for GIA Publications, and he has been a music editorial intern at Oxford University Press. He is currently the Upper School Choral Director at Léman Manhattan Preparatory School in New York City.

I would like to thank Frank Abrahams, Heeyoung Kim, Shaun Holland, Scott Hoerl, Boris Villic, and many other mentors I encountered at Westminster Choir College and Rider University for the incredible opportunities they afforded me during my time there. Thank you to James Jordan and Alec Harris at GIA as well as Norm Hirschy, Lisbeth Redfield, Suzanne Ryan, Adam Cohen, and Jessen O'Brien at Oxford University Press for allowing me to learn and grow on the job under their stellar guidance. Many thanks to Lisa Nowicki for her constant support and to all those at Sanford School who have helped me throughout the years. I am so grateful for the guidance of everyone at Léman Manhattan and Meritas. A huge thank you to everyone at Packt Publishing, especially, Joanne Fitzpatrick, Swati Kumari, Priya Singh, Venu Manthena, Nachiket Vartak, and Mohammad Rizvi. Finally, thank you my amazing parents, siblings, nieces and nephews, and Joshua for your unending care and support.

About the Reviewers

Deb Cook has more than a decade of experience in the classroom and is still that teacher who lives and loves the part. Being equal parts costume, dance, rap/song, and crazed energy, she tries to do it all for her precious lambs.

Her passion is to instill science literacy in our youth through meaningful 21st century avenues of engagement. This was the driving force behind the development of the Biomonsters experience (http://www.biomonsters.com). If her kids love it, she does it with gusto!

She currently teaches science in a brick and mortar high school in Charlottesville, Virginia and in the virtual environment using the Canvas LMS.

Elizabeth Dennis is an instructional designer and trainer for Instructure Canvas. With an in-depth knowledge of quality instructional design for online courses and an expert-level knowledge of Canvas LMS, she has developed a wide variety of courses for K-12, university, and corporate clients. She has published papers in the area of asynchronous instructional design and presented at national conferences on the subject.

Elizabeth is pursuing a Doctorate of Education in Leadership in Higher Education and holds a Master of Education degree with emphasis on educational technology and computer-assisted learning.

Travis Thurston is an Instructional Designer in the Center for Innovative Design & Instruction (CIDI) at Utah State University. He began his career teaching high school history and physical education courses. After earning a Master of Educational Technology degree from Boise State University, he found a new passion in online learning and curriculum development.

At USU, Travis works collaboratively with the team at CIDI to design and redevelop online courses in Instructure Canvas, consult with SMEs on campus to develop and deliver quality courseware, and find practical solutions to various design and delivery challenges. His interests also include utilizing learner analytics in curriculum design and implementing competency-based learning for online programs. Recently, he has written articles about the work done by the team at CIDI, which have been posted on eLearning Industry, eCampus News, and Edudemic.

Donna Harp Ziegenfuss is an Associate Librarian and Assistant Head of Scholarship & Education Services in the J. Willard Marriott Library at the University of Utah. She has an Ed.D. in Academic Leadership/Higher Education and an MS degree in Applied Technology/Instructional Design. She has led Faculty Development Centers and Teaching with Technology Centers, and currently works in the library, focusing on the topics of instructional design, assessment, research, and library instruction projects.

She has over 10 years of experience teaching in traditional, hybrid, and online formats. In addition, she has 15 years of experience working in the area of faculty and professional development. Her research interests focus on library and technology-based instructional planning and course design, assessment topics, faculty and professional development, qualitative research, and academic leadership. She has presented and published technology and teaching-related topics including course design and leadership.

www.PacktPub.com

Support files, eBooks, discount offers, and more

You might want to visit www.PacktPub.com for support files and downloads related to your book.

Did you know that Packt offers eBook versions of every book published, with PDF and ePub files available? You can upgrade to the eBook version at www.PacktPub.com and as a print book customer, you are entitled to a discount on the eBook copy. Get in touch with us at service@packtpub.com for more details.

At www.PacktPub.com, you can also read a collection of free technical articles, sign up for a range of free newsletters, and receive exclusive discounts and offers on Packt books and eBooks.

http://PacktLib.PacktPub.com

Do you need instant solutions to your IT questions? PacktLib is Packt's online digital book library. Here, you can access, read, and search across Packt's entire library of books.

Why subscribe?

- Fully searchable across every book published by Packt
- Copy and paste, print, and bookmark content
- On demand and accessible via web browser

Free access for Packt account holders

If you have an account with Packt at www.PacktPub.com, you can use this to access PacktLib today and view nine entirely free books. Simply use your login credentials for immediate access.

Table of Contents

Preface

Welcome to *Canvas LMS Course Design*! This book will introduce you to Instructure Canvas as a learning management system designed to serve your needs. As citizens of the digital age, we are constantly surrounded by the influx and outflow of new and innovative technologies. We see new devices being introduced, new ideas materialize into software or hardware, and technological trends come and go. In recent decades, one of the most powerful technological trends to reach the field of education is the development of distance learning. For people around the world, the Internet has rapidly increased access to information and knowledge that was once only available to a select few. With technology growing increasingly sophisticated, people everywhere are able to access a world of information in an instant. These developments in accessibility have caused a stir in the field of formal education, which was once one of the only places such information could be found.

As a result of the incredible advances in technology over the recent decades, many of us in the field of education have worked to find ways of harnessing technology and utilizing it within our classrooms. Students' means of finding and interacting with information have been evolving; in contemporary education, there have been numerous advances in the integration of technological developments with the changing paradigms. One such advance is the development of learning management systems (LMSs) to connect students, teachers, and information through technology. First appearing in their current form in the 1990s, LMSs allowed educators to harness the power of the Internet to disseminate course content to students remotely. These systems began to gain popularity in schools worldwide and quickly began to reveal the enormous potential of distance learning and online education.

In the beginning of the 21st century, web-based media also began to expand and develop rapidly with the advent of contemporary social media sites. In a market driven by ease of use and functionalities for users, these social media sites began to integrate tools and features from across the Web with their interfaces to connect users quickly and efficiently across various online platforms. As these features developed and thrived in the realm of social media across the Web, computer scientists Devlin Daley and Brian Whitmer from Brigham Young University in Provo, Utah, saw a need to integrate this ease of use in LMSs. In 2008, they founded Instructure with the mission of creating an LMS with an intuitive, functional, and integrated user interface that would capitalize on the technological skills users already possessed — they called it Canvas (`http://www.deseretnews.com/article/700040784/BYU-grads-introduce-education-savvy-software.html`).

In the six years since its inception, Canvas by Instructure has become the LMS for over 700 institutions with millions of users (`http://www.instructure.com/about-us`). Institutions that adopted Canvas as a replacement for other systems have reported increased engagement with the LMS by students and faculty as well as a reduced number of support tickets (`https://www.youtube.com/watch?v=NbqNxsPMRz4#t=167`). Working to capitalize on the technological skills and expectations of their clientele, the designers of Canvas have not only incorporated elements and ideas from popular services across the Web into the design and features of Canvas, but have also partnered with those services to streamline and integrate users' online experience with the Canvas interface.

This book covers the use of Canvas as a powerful and revolutionary tool for education, both in the traditional classroom and a virtual learning environment. The early chapters of the book explain the setup of your Canvas experience, from setting up your personal profile to designing and building your first course. Taking cues from contemporary social media sites, Canvas allows you to configure your account in the same way you would with other social media accounts — you can add a profile picture, input important information about yourself, and customize the way you interact with Canvas notifications. As you add content to your course, Canvas utilizes text and content editing tools similar to those popular in word processing programs and blogging sites across the Web. With these tools, as well as the other layout and design features built into Canvas, you will have no problem finding the best way to present the content of your course, regardless of your comfort level or experience with web design. Whether you're a novice when it comes to creating content online, an expert in HTML code, or somewhere in between, you can choose from an array of presentation options to display your content without feeling overwhelmed or limited.

The second half of this book is focused on using Canvas to teach your course. Stemming from the tools and functions of a traditional live classroom—grade books, due dates, class meetings, and office hours—Canvas has transformed each of these tools and functions for use in the digital age. In addition to these basic features, Canvas offers a range of special features including a mobile application, learning outcomes and rubrics, web-based apps, and a Course Analytics feature. These features allow users to differentiate their own Canvas experience in the same way you differentiate learning activities for your students. As you work your way through your first experience with Canvas, questions are bound to arise. While this book seeks to predict and answer many of those questions, Canvas offers a phenomenal built-in user support system. Based directly on users' questions and concerns, Canvas Guides offers you a searchable wealth of information including video tutorials, step-by-step instructions, and frequently asked questions.

With all of the skills you will have gained from your first experience with Canvas over the course of this book, it is up to you to be a part of the educational revolution that can change the world (http://www.instructure.com/about-us). Exploring the Framework for 21st Century Learning as advocated by the Partnership for 21st Century Skills, the closing sections of this book offer specific suggestions for Canvas to engage many of the skills necessary for contemporary learners to succeed. These suggestions are intended to serve as fodder for your own creative explorations of Canvas, using it as a tool to enhance teaching and foster students' success.

As a product, Canvas has been designed to meet the unique needs of its users within contemporary education. As a powerful educational tool, Canvas opens the door to countless possibilities for you and the students you teach as citizens of the digital age.

What this book covers

Chapter 1, Getting Started with Canvas, addresses how to create a Canvas course, navigate Canvas, and set up your Canvas profile, including contact information and notification preferences.

Chapter 2, Building Your Canvas Course, guides you through building your course with in-depth, step-by-step guidance through the features of Canvas to successfully begin course construction by working through the integrated Course Setup Checklist.

Chapter 3, Getting Ready to Launch Your Course, continues along the Course Setup Checklist with a focus on organization and presentation of the course once the bulk of the content has been created. You will have your course built and published by the end of this chapter.

Chapter 4, Teaching Your Canvas Course, explains how to use the features of Canvas to enhance your teaching once your course begins. You will learn how to communicate with students through messaging, provide feedback on assignments, and use the grading and assessment tools offered by Canvas.

Chapter 5, Exploring Special Features, addresses special features and unique extras that Canvas offers such as the Canvas mobile app, outcomes and rubrics, registered services, apps, and more involved Canvas functions such as the Course Analytics system.

Chapter 6, Where to Go for Help, offers guidance on where to obtain help with Canvas. It covers how to access Canvas Guides and the option of contacting your institution's IT department for help with institution-specific Canvas sites.

Chapter 7, Now You're Ready!, offers a summary of the key points encountered during the course-building process, along with connections to educational philosophies and practices that support technology as a powerful way to enhance teaching and learning.

Appendix, References and Resources, offers information on materials referenced throughout this book and other resources that you might find helpful as you learn and grow as an online educator.

What you need for this book

For this book, you will need the following:

- A computer
- Reliable Internet access
- A webcam and a microphone
- Your course syllabus and materials (for example, readings, handouts, and videos)

If your institution uses Canvas, you may also need the following:

- The Canvas URL specific to your institution
- Your institution's login information
- The contact information for your institution's IT department

Who this book is for

This book will be of use to the following:

- Educators who use or are learning to use Canvas to house content for their courses
- Teacher's assistants who use or are learning to use Canvas to facilitate a class
- Individuals in charge of designing and building a Canvas course
- Administrators interested in the features of Canvas as an LMS

Conventions

In this book, you will find a number of styles of text that distinguish between different kinds of information. Here are some examples of these styles, and an explanation of their meaning.

Code words in text, database table names, folder names, filenames, file extensions, pathnames, dummy URLs, user input, and Twitter handles are shown as follows: "Files with a .zip extension contain a file or group of files that have been compressed for easy transportation between programs or devices."

New terms and **important words** are shown in bold. Words that you see on the screen, in menus or dialog boxes for example, appear in the text like this: "Click on **Save** to create your assignment."

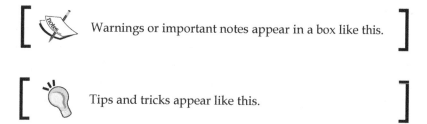

Warnings or important notes appear in a box like this.

Tips and tricks appear like this.

Reader feedback

Feedback from our readers is always welcome. Let us know what you think about this book—what you liked or may have disliked. Reader feedback is important for us to develop titles that you really get the most out of.

To send us general feedback, simply send an e-mail to feedback@packtpub.com, and mention the book title via the subject of your message.

If there is a topic that you have expertise in and you are interested in either writing or contributing to a book, see our author guide on www.packtpub.com/authors.

Customer support

Now that you are the proud owner of a Packt book, we have a number of things to help you to get the most from your purchase.

Errata

Although we have taken every care to ensure the accuracy of our content, mistakes do happen. If you find a mistake in one of our books—maybe a mistake in the text or the code—we would be grateful if you would report this to us. By doing so, you can save other readers from frustration and help us improve subsequent versions of this book. If you find any errata, please report them by visiting http://www.packtpub.com/submit-errata, selecting your book, clicking on the **errata submission form** link, and entering the details of your errata. Once your errata are verified, your submission will be accepted and the errata will be uploaded on our website, or added to any list of existing errata, under the Errata section of that title. Any existing errata can be viewed by selecting your title from http://www.packtpub.com/support.

Piracy

Piracy of copyright material on the Internet is an ongoing problem across all media. At Packt, we take the protection of our copyright and licenses very seriously. If you come across any illegal copies of our works, in any form, on the Internet, please provide us with the location address or website name immediately so that we can pursue a remedy.

Please contact us at copyright@packtpub.com with a link to the suspected pirated material.

We appreciate your help in protecting our authors, and our ability to bring you valuable content.

Questions

You can contact us at questions@packtpub.com if you are having a problem with any aspect of the book, and we will do our best to address it.

1
Getting Started with Canvas

In this chapter, we will cover how to access **Canvas** and navigate the home screen, which is called the dashboard. Once you have learned your way around the site, you will learn how to set up your Canvas profile, enter your contact information, adjust your general settings, and configure your notification preferences. Next, we will learn how to create a Canvas course, specifically, how to create a course yourself versus how to begin participating in a course that has been set up by your institution. Once we have created your course, we will be ready to move on to building your course in the next chapter.

A wide range of institutions across the world use Canvas as their institutional **learning management system (LMS)**. In addition, Canvas is usable in a variety of learning situations outside of traditional institutions. To accommodate the different situations in which users may find themselves while teaching or learning, Canvas offers two types of accounts.

Types of Canvas accounts

To get started, let's discuss the two types of Canvas accounts that you may encounter.

Institution-specific Canvas accounts

If the college, university, or K-12 school that you work for uses Canvas for its LMS, you will most likely receive information from the Information Technology (IT) department or an administrator regarding the best ways to access and use Canvas. When Canvas is fully integrated into a university's enrollment and course registration system, for example, you may likely be able to log in using the same username and password you use to access your school e-mail account. In addition, once you log in, you may find that the IT department has enabled or disabled certain settings to maintain consistency for the institution. Each situation is slightly different, so reach out to someone in the IT or administrative departments to find out specific information for your school.

Free for Teachers Canvas accounts

Canvas offers a **Free for Teachers** account for educators who do not have access to Canvas through an institution. This account allows you to register using any e-mail address, then create and build courses that you would like to teach, regardless of whether you work for an institution that uses Canvas as its LMS. We will go over how to set up a Free for Teachers account in the next section, where we will begin with a discussion of how to access Canvas. As a note, all examples and screenshots in this book are taken from a Free for Teachers account.

Accessing Canvas and creating your account

To begin, open your web browser (for example, Internet Explorer, Safari, Google Chrome, or Mozilla Firefox). If you are using an institution-specific Canvas site, consult any information you have received from your school, specifically looking for the URL (web address) for your school's Canvas site. After we address how to log in for institutional Canvas accounts, we will cover how to access and log in to a Free for Teachers account.

Accessing your institution's Canvas site

To access your institution's Canvas site, perform the following steps:

1. Open your web browser and enter the URL for your institution's Canvas site.

2. You can also copy and paste the URL from any informational e-mails you may have received from your institution. While your institution's Canvas URL may follow a variety of formats, a common formula for the institutional Canvas URL is `http://institution.instructure.com` in which you will enter the actual name of your school instead of "institution".

3. If you have instructions from the IT or administrative team at your school, follow those instructions to set up your account. As mentioned previously, each situation is slightly different, so you may need to get support for your specific case if you have questions.

Often, you will receive an e-mail invitation to join Canvas that includes a link to follow and clear step-by-step instructions once you follow the link to Canvas. In other cases, the institutional ID that you use to access your school e-mail account or registration system may automatically be carried over to Canvas, depending on how your school has integrated Canvas with the rest of their management systems.

In most cases, if your institution uses Canvas as its LMS, you do not need to create a Free for Teachers account. However, consult members of your institution's IT or administrative department for specific instructions if you are not sure.

Creating a Free for Teachers account

The following steps will walk you through how to create your own Free for Teachers account within Canvas:

1. To create a Free for Teachers account, open your web browser and navigate to canvas.instructure.com.

2. When the page loads, click on **Need a Canvas account? Click here, it's free!** and you will be taken to a registration page.

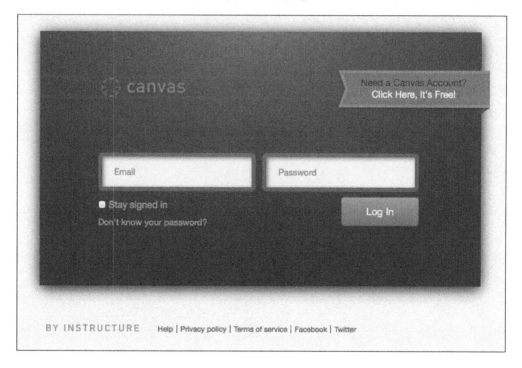

3. Select whether you are a **Teacher**, **Student**, or **Parent** from the **Title** drop-down menu.

4. Then, fill in your information on the registration screen, take a look at **terms of use** and **privacy policy**, check the **You agree to the terms of use and acknowledge the privacy policy** checkbox, and click on the blue box at the bottom-right corner of the window. This box will read **Start Teaching**, **Start Learning**, or **Start Participating** depending on whether you are a teacher, student, or parent. The following screenshot displays what you will see when you create an account as a **Teacher**:

5. Once you submit your registration, you will receive a confirmation e-mail as well as a welcome e-mail. The confirmation e-mail will include a link that you must follow to complete your registration and create your password.

6. Once you have followed the e-mail link to confirm your registration, you can log in at `http://canvas.instructure.com` again using your e-mail address and a new password to begin using Canvas!

Navigating Canvas – the dashboard

When you log in for the first time, you will be taken to the Canvas dashboard. There are four main sections of the dashboard, which we'll familiarize ourselves with now, then go into more detail as we learn about what you can do within each section of Canvas:

1. In the top-right corner of the dashboard, you will see your name, **Inbox**, **Settings**, **Logout**, and **Help**. This menu, shown in the following screenshot, will usually be visible to you regardless of the page you are viewing in Canvas:

2. Along the top-left side of the screen, you will see the Canvas logo (or your institution's logo), and a list of tabs that read **Home**, **Assignments**, **Grades**, and **Calendar**. Once you get started with your course or courses, the **Home** link will turn into a **Courses** link with a drop-down menu. This top menu will also usually be visible to you on any page you are viewing in Canvas, and you can always access your Canvas dashboard by clicking on the logo in the top-left corner, as seen in the following screenshot:

3. In the center of the dashboard, you will see a **Welcome to Canvas!** message, a message with a **Configure Communication Preferences** button to configure the communication preferences, and a **Recent Activity** section at the bottom. The **Recent Activity** section functions like the Newsfeed on Facebook or the Twitter feed on Twitter. Eventually, this section of your dashboard will display items such as announcements that have been posted in courses, messages that have been sent to you, and assignments that have been submitted to your courses. The **Recent Activity** section is a quick and easy way to check what has happened in your courses while you've been away from your computer. This section, which only appears on the Canvas dashboard, is shown in the following screenshot:

Welcome to Canvas!
You don't have any courses, so this page won't be very exciting for now. Once you've created or signed up for courses, you'll start to see conversations from all of your classes.

Configure Communication Preferences
Now that you're registered with Canvas, you might want to configure what notifications you'll receive as your courses progress. Canvas is flexible enough to let you choose how and for what events you'd like to be notified. When things happen in your courses you can choose to be emailed or texted to your cell immediately, daily or weekly.

Configure Communication Preferences

Recent Activity

4. The **Coming Up** section on the right side of your screen will eventually be filled with helpful reminders about what's coming up on the calendars for all of your courses:

   ° You can click on **View Calendar** to see a calendar layout of what's going on in all of your courses including assignment due dates, online meetings, and more.

   ° Once your courses are up and running, you will also see a **To Do** list displayed above the **Coming Up** section. The **To Do** list will show you any assignments that need to be graded for any of your courses along with the number of submissions that need to be graded.

○ You will also see a **Start a New Course** button that will allow you to start a new course under the **Coming Up** section. We will get to this button soon, but as you can guess, this is the button you will click on to create a brand new course. This section, as displayed in the following screenshot, also only appears on the dashboard:

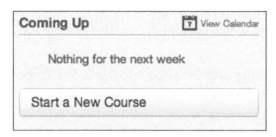

Another helpful section to notice is the menu at the very bottom of the screen. This menu includes links to **Help**, **Privacy policy**, **Terms of service**, **Facebook**, and **Twitter**. These links are useful guides to general information about **Instructure** as a company and your usage of Canvas. The **Help** link that appears in this menu will take you to the same page as the **Help** link in the top-right menu. The bottom menu, shown in the following screenshot, will usually be visible to you on any page you are viewing within Canvas:

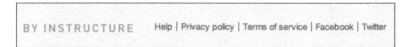

Now that you're familiar with the basic layout of the Canvas dashboard, let's work through how to set up your personal settings and communication preferences.

Adjusting your profile, settings, and notifications

In this section, we will address how to set up your Canvas profile, adjust your general account settings, and personalize your notification settings. If you are using an institutional account, the ability to adjust your profile, settings, and notifications may be limited or different than described in this section. While your individual situation may vary, let's start by covering how to set up your Canvas profile, which other users will see as they interact with you on Canvas.

Adjusting your profile

Your Canvas profile includes your profile picture, biography, and website links. To begin, perform the following steps:

1. Click on your name in the top-right menu of the dashboard.

2. This will bring you to your profile page. Your profile page is a part of your account settings, which are laid out similarly to the way Canvas courses are laid out.

Your other account settings appear on the left-side menu as shown in the following screenshot, but for now, let's update your profile picture:

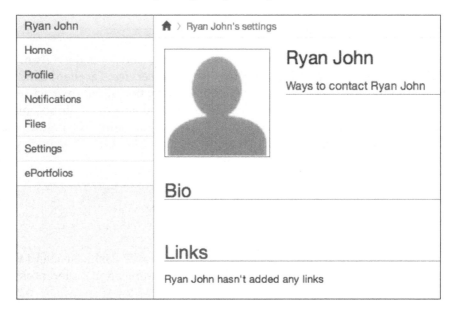

Adding a profile picture

Including a photo of yourself makes your presence on Canvas immediately more relatable and inviting. When participants can see a photo of someone who is writing to them or is posting on discussion boards, the Canvas community becomes more vibrant, personalized, and engaging. To add or change your profile picture, perform the following steps:

1. Click on the gray outline of a person next to your name on your profile page. Notice that when you hover your mouse over this gray image, an icon appears in the bottom-right part of the image that looks like a pencil. This pencil icon is the symbol for editing something within Canvas, so in most situations, you can click on the pencil icon wherever you see it in order to edit what you're looking at. In the following screenshot, you see an example of the gray outline as well as the editing pencil icon seen throughout Canvas:

2. After you click on the pencil icon, a pop-up window will appear with three options along the top side: **Upload a Picture**, **Take a Picture**, and **From Gravatar**.

3. To upload a photo from your computer, click on **Upload a Picture** and then click on **choose a picture** below it.

4. From there, another pop-up window will appear, which will allow you to select the image you would like to use as your profile picture from your computer. Once you have found the picture on your computer, click on the file and then click on **Open**.

5. Next, you can crop the picture into a square using the cropping tools that appear. After you have cropped your photo, click on **Save** and your picture will be updated. The following screenshot displays the cropping tools as well as the **Save** button:

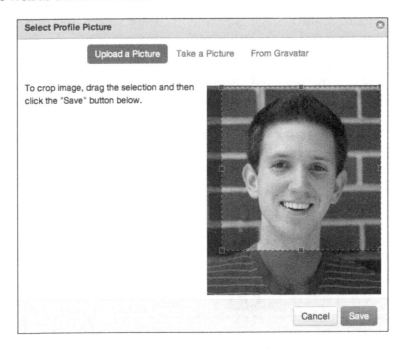

6. If you click on **Take a Picture** at the top of the pop-up window, your webcam will open and you will be able to take a new photo to use as your profile picture.

7. If you have a Gravatar account (a separate account from Canvas), you can click on **From Gravatar** to select your profile picture from your Gravatar account.

8. After you click on the **Save** button, the profile picture window will close and you will see that the image you selected has replaced the default gray outline profile picture as displayed in the following screenshot:

Editing your profile

To edit what other Canvas users can see about you, you can adjust your name, title, and bio, as well as add links to your personal or professional websites. As with your profile picture, any information you add to your Canvas profile will help participants gain a better understanding of who you are as a person. Within a fully online learning environment, establishing personal connections with participants can be very important in building a productive and comfortable learning community. To add information to your profile, perform the following steps:

1. Begin on your profile page and click on **Edit Profile** on the right side of the screen.

2. This will open editing boxes for your **Name**, **Title**, **Bio**, and **Links** fields. You can click on each editing box to adjust or add content.

3. When you are finished editing, click on **Save Profile** at the bottom of the screen before moving on, as shown in the following screenshot:

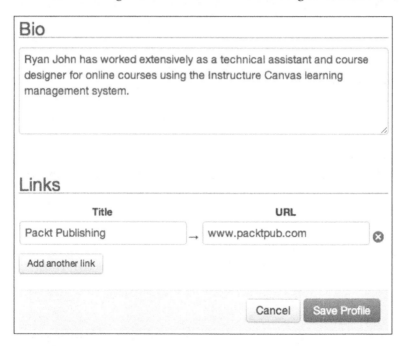

Once you have saved your updates, they will be visible to other Canvas users when they view your profile. You may notice a message under the **Ways to Contact Me** section that mentions you have not registered any services. Next, we will learn how to adjust your account settings and add alternative forms of contact including e-mail addresses, cell phone numbers, or registered services such as Facebook, Twitter, Skype, or LinkedIn.

Adjusting your account settings

To adjust your account settings such as your display name, contact information, language, time zone, and integrated web services, click on the **Settings** link in the top-right menu:

You can also access your settings by clicking on the **Settings** link on the left-side menu of your profile page. Let's begin by adjusting your contact information so anything you receive from Canvas goes to an address, device, or program that you check frequently.

Adding a new e-mail address

On your **Settings** page, the **Ways to Contact** section on the right-side menu includes the e-mail address with which you have registered and the option to add more e-mail addresses as well as more methods of contact. To add an e-mail address, perform the following steps:

1. Click on the **Add Email Address** link.
2. A pop-up window will appear that will let you add as many alternate e-mail addresses as you would like, with the option of signing in to Canvas with any of them.
3. If you would like to sign in to Canvas using a new e-mail, type in the new e-mail address, check the box next to **I want to log in to Canvas using this email address**, and then click on **Register Email** in the bottom-right corner of the pop-up window, as shown in the following screenshot:

Once you click on **Register Email**, the pop-up window will close and you can continue editing your contact information.

Adding a cell phone number for SMS text notifications

One of the unique features of Canvas is the ability to receive notifications from Canvas directly to your cell phone. Depending on your desired level of availability to participants and how frequently you would like to monitor activity with your courses, you may choose to add your cell phone number and receive notifications via SMS texts. For example, this feature might be a wise option if you consistently check your cell phone but rarely check your e-mail. To add your cell phone number in order to receive SMS text message notifications, perform the following steps:

1. Click on **Add Contact Method** under the **Ways to Contact** section on the right-side menu of the **Settings** page.

2. In the pop-up window, enter your cell phone number and select your provider. The SMS e-mail address should automatically appear once you select your provider. Note that Canvas SMS services are currently geared toward US providers.

3. Once you have entered your number and selected your provider, click on **Register SMS** in the bottom-right corner of the pop-up window, as shown in the following screenshot:

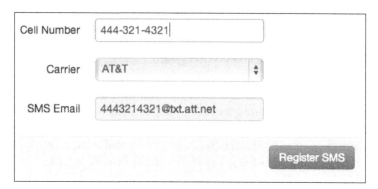

4. You will then see a new pop-up window (next screenshot) appear in your browser that asks for a confirmation code. You should receive an SMS text on your cell phone with the confirmation code, which you should then enter into the pop-up window on your screen and click on **Confirm**. If you do not receive an SMS text with a confirmation number and you entered your phone number correctly, click on the **Re-Send Confirmation** link in the pop-up window. If you entered your number incorrectly, close the pop-up window and begin the process again by clicking on **Add Contact Method** under the **Ways to Contact** section on the right-side menu of the **Settings** page:

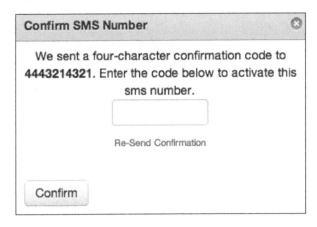

5. Once you have confirmed your cell phone number, you will be able to receive notifications via text messages.

Editing your general settings

As with many other online services you may have encountered, configuring the general settings of your Canvas account is important for proper and accurate functioning of your account. Your general settings include your name, preferred language, current time zone, and password. Also found within the general settings menu are the options to receive Instructure informational e-mails and delete your account. To edit your general settings, perform the following steps:

1. Navigate to the main **Settings** page.
2. On the right-side menu, click on the **Edit Settings** button underneath the **Ways to Contact** menu as shown in the following screenshot:

3. You will see textboxes and drop-down menus appear in the center part of the screen. When adjusting the **Full Name**, **Display Name**, and **Sortable Name** fields for your account, each section includes a brief description of where that display name will appear. For example, if you are teaching a college course, you may want your name to be displayed with the title of `Professor` or `Dr.` for discussion posts, messages, and comments. The following screenshot provides an example of each type of name:

Full Name:	Ryan John
	This name will be used for grading.
Display Name:	Mr. John
	People will see this name in discussions, messages and comments.
Sortable Name:	John, Ryan
	This name appears in sorted lists.

4. Below your name settings, you can use the **Language** and **Time Zone** drop-down menus to adjust the language of your Canvas experience as well as the time zone in which you live. To adjust your time zone, click on the drop-down menu and select from the listed options.

5. You can check the box next to **I want to receive information, news and tips from Instructure**, as shown in the following screenshot, if you would like Instructure to e-mail you about certain features of Canvas. You will not receive informational product e-mails from Instructure if you do not check this box, though you will receive course notification e-mails based on your notification settings:

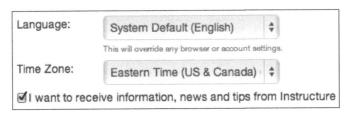

6. To change your password, check the box next to **Change Password** and a new menu will open below that checkbox.

7. Using the drop-down menu that appears, select the e-mail address you would like to change the password for, then enter your old password, your new password, and confirm your new password in the appropriate boxes as shown in the following screenshot:

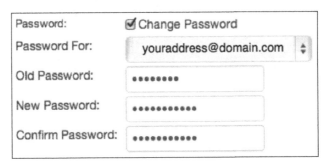

8. When finished, click on the blue **Update Settings** box below your settings information.

The option to delete your account also appears within the menu to edit your general settings. To delete your account, perform the following steps:

1. Navigate to the the main **Settings** page and click on the **Edit Settings** button underneath the **Ways to Contact** menu.

2. Scroll down and click on the red **Delete My Account** link.

3. You will be taken to a new page that asks if you really want to delete your account. If you are positive you would like to delete your account, click on the button that says **Delete [Your Name]** and your account will be permanently deleted, as shown in the following screenshot:

Moving on from your general account settings, let's explore some of the innovative connections you can configure between Canvas and other common online services, referred to as **Registered Services**.

Using registered services

Canvas allows you to link registered services to your Canvas account in order to better integrate Canvas into your life online. Utilizing **Registered Services** allows you to connect Canvas to other websites, programs, and networks you already use when you are online. Again, if you are using an institutional account, your options for external services may be limited or different compared to those discussed in this section. If you already have accounts with any of the services seen in the following screenshot, you can link your Canvas profile to your external accounts to utilize the features of those external services:

To connect the preceding services to your Canvas account as registered services, perform the following steps:

1. Click on the service you would like to link to your Canvas account.

2. Each service has slightly different instructions that appear, so follow the onscreen instructions carefully to link your Canvas account to your external service account.

3. Once you have linked Canvas to one of the listed services, that service will appear under the **Registered Services** heading, as shown in the following screenshot:

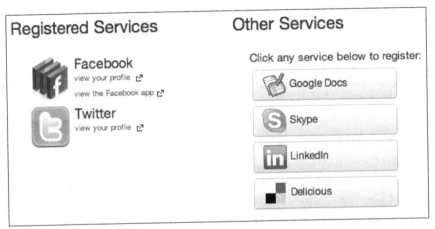

One of the most common reasons to register an external service with Canvas is to receive Canvas notifications while you are logged in to that external service. To adjust these options, let's now discuss how to customize your notification preferences.

Customizing your notification preferences

Your notification preferences are some of the most important things to know how to adjust when using Canvas. The same goes for your students, since not being notified of an announcement or a direct message could mean missing an online meeting or assignment if their notification preferences are not adjusted appropriately. The easiest way to access your notification settings is to click on **Notifications** on the left menu of your account **Settings** page. If you've just added a profile picture, updated your profile, and edited your general account settings, look to the left of your screen and click on **Notifications**, as shown in the following screenshot:

The **Notifications** page allows you to adjust the following:

- Which activities you receive notifications about (for example, due dates, inbox messages, or announcements)
- How will you receive notifications (for example, via e-mail, text, Facebook, or Twitter)
- When will you receive notifications (for example, immediately, daily, weekly, or never)

When you open your **Notification Preferences**, you will see a spreadsheet-like grid, shown in the following screenshot, which lists the course activities you can be notified about in the left column and the method of notification along the top row:

Notification Preferences

Course Activities	Email Address yourname@domain.com	Facebook Ryan John
Due Date	Weekly	Weekly
Grading Policies	Daily	ASAP
Course Content	Weekly	Daily
Files	Weekly	Weekly
Announcement	ASAP	ASAP

The methods of notification along the top come from the contact information and the registered services that you have configured in your general account settings. You will notice that in the center of the grid, you can hover your mouse over the cross sections of **Course Activities** and your chosen methods of contact. If you hover your mouse over any of these cross sections, you can select one of the four options for how frequently Canvas will notify you about the selected activity. The following screenshots show each option:

To adjust your notification preferences, perform the following steps:

1. Locate the course activity you would like to be notified about.
2. Then, find the method of contact through which you would like to be notified about that activity.

3. Within the **Notification Preferences** grid, click on one of the four notification frequency options to set the notification method and frequency. For example, the following screenshot displays the **Send daily summary** option to send a daily summary for any changes to **Grading Policies**:

4. Once you have selected the notification frequency, you will see an icon with the selected frequency show up on the grid.

5. Your notification preferences are automatically saved once you select them.

As you become more familiar with Canvas and begin participating in courses, you may decide to return to your notification settings once you have a better idea of your needs and preferences.

Now that we've covered all of the basics of setting up your profile, adjusting your settings, and customizing your notification preferences, let's get started with creating your course!

Creating your Canvas course

As mentioned at the beginning of this chapter, your Canvas account will fall under the umbrella of an institutional Canvas account or a Free for Teachers account. Creating a course is different for both types of accounts, and you may find that your specific institution's Canvas situation might be a hybrid of both, depending on how your school has chosen to integrate Canvas with its other systems. To begin, let's start with how to access your new blank course if it has been set up by your institution's IT or other administrative department.

Joining a course created by your institution

If your school uses Canvas as its LMS, you will mostly likely not need to deal with the initial creation of your Canvas course. In fact, you may not have the ability to create your own Canvas course; in this case, you will need to go through your IT or administrative department to create a course within your institution's Canvas site. Often, the IT or administrative department will have all of your courses created automatically when they create the course within the institutional course registration system.

When courses are created automatically, you will often also be automatically added to those courses, at which point they will appear when you log in to Canvas without any action on your part. Alternately, if your IT team manually creates your course, you will receive an e-mail inviting you to officially join the course. After the IT or administrative teams have created your course, you will receive an e-mail that informs you that you have been invited to participate in your course as a teacher. The following screenshot is a sample of what the e-mail may contain:

Instructure Canvas   November 13, 2013 8:13 PM
To: Ryan John <   Details
Course Invitation   All Mail - Google

> You've been invited to participate in the course, Canvas LMS
> Course Design, as a teacher.
>
> Name: **Ryan John**
> Email: youremail@domain.com
>
> Click here to view the course page

From there, you should follow the link in the main body of the e-mail:

1. You will be directed to the Canvas login page for your institution, where you should log in using your institutional username and password or the username and password you set up with your IT or other administrative department.

2. Once you log in, your dashboard should include **Decline** or **Accept** buttons to decline or accept the course invitation. Once you click on **Accept**, the course will show up on the top-left menu under the **Courses** link.

3. From there, you can click on **Courses**, select the course you have just joined, and begin the course building process that we will cover in *Chapter 2, Building Your Canvas Course*.

If you are not using Canvas through an institution, you will need to create a course using your Free for Teachers account.

Creating a new course with a Free for Teachers account

If you are using the Free for Teachers version of Canvas, you can create a new course from your dashboard. For institutional account users, you may also have this option depending on how your IT team has configured Canvas. To create a new course, perform the following steps:

1. Navigate to your Canvas dashboard.

2. On the right-side menu, click on the button that says **Start a New Course**.

3. From there, a pop-up window will appear within your browser. In that window, you can name your course, assign an abbreviation and course number, select the content license from a drop-down menu, and choose whether you would like the course to be publicly accessible. In most cases, you will probably want to keep your course private, but you may choose whichever option is most applicable to your unique course situation.

4. Once you have entered all the information for your course, click on **Create course**.

The following screenshot shows you how the pop-up window will look like and offers examples of what you might want to include when setting up your course:

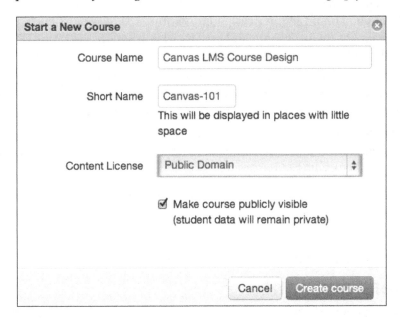

Your course is now created! After you click on **Create course**, you will be taken to the home page of your new course. You'll notice that the course layout is similar to what we saw while editing your account settings. We will go over how to navigate your course in more detail throughout the rest of the book, but you should see that:

- The top-right menu is still visible and unchanged
- The top-left menu is still visible and unchanged
- The left-side menu lists specific locations and options within the course
- The center of the screen displays the main content of the course home page
- The right-side menu displays the **Coming Up** section along with the option to post a new announcement
- The bottom menu is still visible and unchanged

Also, note that a course checklist hovers at the bottom of the screen. This checklist will walk you through the various steps in adding content to and publishing your course.

When you create your course, it will remain unpublished until you choose to publish it. Until your course is published, only teachers, designers, and teacher's assistants (TAs) that have been added to the course will be able to access the course content. Once the course is published, students you have added to the course will be able to access the course content. You will see the message displayed in the following screenshot when your course is unpublished:

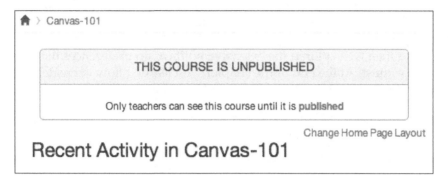

Depending on how you would like your course to run, it is up to you when you decide to officially publish your course and allow all participants to access the content. In later chapters, we will cover how to control exactly what participants can see within your course once it is published, but at this point it is probably best to wait until you have finished designing your course before officially publishing it.

Now that we have created your first course, we can begin building the course by adding and organizing content in the coming chapters.

Summary

At the beginning of this chapter, we discussed the different types of Canvas accounts you might encounter. We discussed how to set up and access an institutional Canvas account and a Free for Teachers Canvas account, and then we moved on to navigate Canvas once we logged in. After examining the various menus of the Canvas dashboard, we covered how to edit your profile, including how to add a profile picture, and update your bio and links. From there, we learned how to adjust your account settings including contact information, your display name, preferred language, and time zone. We worked through how to change your password and what to do if you need to delete your account for any reason. Next, we covered how to link registered services to your accounts such as Facebook, Twitter, Skype, and LinkedIn, and then we explored the extensive notification preferences that Canvas allows you to adjust. At the end of the chapter, you learned how to create a course, both from an institutional account and a Free for Teachers account perspective.

As we move forward into *Chapter 2, Building Your Canvas Course*, we will dive into adding content to your course and learn how to tailor your Canvas course to meet your needs and the needs of your students.

2

Building Your Canvas Course

This chapter will cover the foundations of building your Canvas course to create and arrange the content your students will interact with when they log in. We will start by exploring the **Course Setup Checklist**, which will help guide you through the process of building your course. We will then discuss some of the important ideas to keep in mind when planning your course and conceptualizing how you will use Canvas for your unique educational situation. After this, we will learn how to import content from another course on Canvas or from another **learning management system (LMS)**. Next, we will work through how to add **assignments** and content to your course, specifically focusing on how to use the **Rich Content Editor**. We will examine the various types of assignments you can create within Canvas, and we will cover how to create assignment groups for weighted assignments.

Exploring the Course Setup Checklist

When you click on your newly created course (remember that it's listed under **Courses** on the top-left menu of the dashboard), you will be taken to the home page of your new course. By default, you will see the **Next Steps** checklist appear at the bottom of your screen with a number of options listed for setting up your course. This checklist is a guide that helps you make sure that all of the essential elements of your course are up and running before you publish the course and allow students to access the content. The **Next Steps** checklist is shown in the following screenshot:

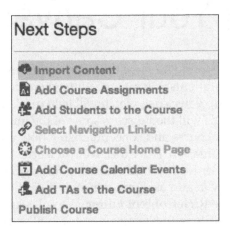

If you hover your mouse over the options in the **Next Steps** checklist, you will notice that a description of each option appears on the right-hand side.

 Throughout Canvas, you can often hover your mouse over links or icons to learn more about how they work and what they do.

If you click on the **X** in the top-right corner of the **Next Steps** checklist, the checklist will disappear from your screen. You may wish to do this once you start designing assignments or content pages so that you can see the full screen more easily. If you wish to get the **Next Steps** checklist to appear again, go to the course's home page and click on **Course Setup Checklist** on the right-side menu above the announcements and calendar, as shown in the following screenshot:

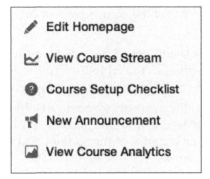

While we will cover everything in the **Next Steps** checklist eventually, this chapter will walk you through the finer details of the first two items of this checklist:

- How to import content
- How to add course assignments and content to your course

Before we dive into actually building your course, let's discuss the planning that should go into designing your course before you start.

Planning your course – from syllabus to screen

As you sit down to think about how to build and organize your Canvas course, there are a number of things to consider that will impact the way you will use Canvas to manage your course content. The following questions and prompts will help you determine the approaches you could consider while building your course:

- What kind of course am I teaching?
    - A traditional live course
    - A fully online course
    - A live course with online expectations (for example, assignment submission, discussion board postings, video assignments, and peer reviews)

- What do I need to do to get the course content into a format that is suitable for Canvas?
  - The course is brand new. I have not taught a live or online version of the course before, so I need to find and sequence the course content before I begin building my Canvas course.
  - I have taught the course previously as a live course. The content is already organized in a syllabus, so the bulk of my work will be to obtain electronic copies of the content and add existing content to my Canvas course.
  - I have taught the course previously as an online course using another LMS. The content is already organized in a syllabus and I have all of the content in an electronic form. I need to import and organize the course content into Canvas.
  - I have taught the course previously, either live or online, using another LMS. The content is already organized in a syllabus, so I will need to obtain electronic copies of the content and import the course content from another LMS.

- What purpose will Canvas serve in the day-to-day life of my course?
  - Canvas will be a *supplement to a live course* where students can access assigned content and communicate with their peers and me.
  - Canvas will be the *sole platform for a fully online course*. Students will interact with all of the content, other students, and me via Canvas.
  - Canvas will *facilitate a variety of live and online assignments/expectations* in addition to housing supplementary content and streamlining communication.

- How will students interact with Canvas?
  - Students will use Canvas as a supplement to the live course in which they are participating. They will have access to a hard copy of everything they need in class, but they can find the same material online as well. They will check Canvas to see their grades for the various assignments that they will turn in to me during class.
  - Students will use Canvas to participate in an online course. They will access the course content, submit assignments electronically, and communicate solely through Canvas.
  - Students will use Canvas for the administrative aspects of their live course. They will access content via Canvas, and they may have the option to submit assignments in the class or electronically. Canvas will connect them in a way that is similar to how they connect over social media sites.

- How will I interact with Canvas?

    ° I will post the material we cover in class on Canvas for students to access remotely (for example, the course syllabus, in-class presentations, class notes, readings, and assignment instructions). I will post grades to Canvas, but I will communicate comments and feedback in person.

    ° I will teach the entire course using Canvas. I will post content for students to explore, facilitate online lectures, collect and grade assignments, and communicate feedback to students via Canvas.

    ° I will use the features of Canvas to enhance the experiences that students have during class. I will post core and supplemental content, create assignments for electronic submission, and communicate with students via Canvas in addition to face-to-face interactions.

Your answers to these questions will vary depending on your situation, and the options listed in the preceding points are only the most common; you may have any combination of the preceding situations present in your workload. A vital aspect of successfully utilizing the capabilities of Canvas is determining what your needs are. Once you determine what you need to accomplish, you can use this book to help you meet your goals.

If you are using Canvas to teach a course that you have taught in the past with an existing syllabus, what you already have is a great place to start. Take the existing syllabus and organize it into sections. Think about the sequence of the content, the various types of projects and assignments, as well as the assessment and grading strategies you have used. Canvas can play as large or small a role as you need for any of these elements of your syllabus based on your answers to the preceding questions.

As an example, let's discuss using electronic versions of your course content. If you need to obtain electronic versions of your course content, check the copyright laws regarding the educational use of materials for your country. In many cases, you may be able to scan content and upload it directly to Canvas. This way, students have instant access to the content directly through Canvas, and you can sequence content within Canvas so students access it in the order you desire. You may alternatively wish to have your students purchase e-book or hard copy editions of your chosen textbooks. Another option still would be to only use traditional hard copies of the content by either distributing copies in class or requiring students to purchase the content on their own. As you become more familiar with the capabilities of Canvas in the coming chapters, you will gain a better understanding of how you would like to use Canvas for your course. However, the more traditional planning you put into your course before you start building it, the easier it will be for you to transition to using Canvas for that course.

As a large number of institutions, especially those in higher education, have adopted and begun to use LMSs in recent years, you have probably encountered another LMS in the time you've spent at your institution. You may have taught courses using these systems in the past. If that's the case, the following section will help you import content from your previous courses in other systems into Canvas. If you are building your course from scratch or have not used another LMS when teaching your course previously, you are welcome to flip through to the following section on adding assignments and content to your course.

Importing content from another course

Though this is the first step of **Course Setup Checklist**, if you are a new Canvas user and are planning to build your Canvas course from scratch, you will most likely want to skip to the next section. If you are importing a course from another LMS, you can find the instructions to do so here, and then you will need to go through the course using information from the rest of the chapter to reformat the course content.

The first step in importing content from another Canvas course or LMS is to export or extract that content from its original host site. Exporting content is different for every LMS, but the option to export an entire course is usually found in the course settings. Consult your IT department or the technology support for the host site if you need help exporting. We will cover how to export a course from Canvas in *Chapter 7, Now You're Ready!* once we have completed building your course. To import content into your course, perform the following steps:

1. Export your course content from its original host site, and then make sure that you save the exported file to an easily accessible location on your computer (for example, your desktop or your My Documents folder).

    One of the most common file formats for an exported course is the .zip file format. Files with a .zip extension contain a file or group of files that have been compressed for easy transportation between programs or devices. Think of it as a suitcase; rather than transporting four outfits individually for a business trip, you zip them all together in a suitcase for easy transportation.

2. Navigate to the home page of your course and look at the **Next Steps** checklist at the bottom of the screen. If you hover your mouse over **Import Content** in the **Next Steps** checklist, look to the right-hand side, and you will notice the following description appear. To begin importing the content, click on the **Import Content** link that appears in the description as shown in the following screenshot:

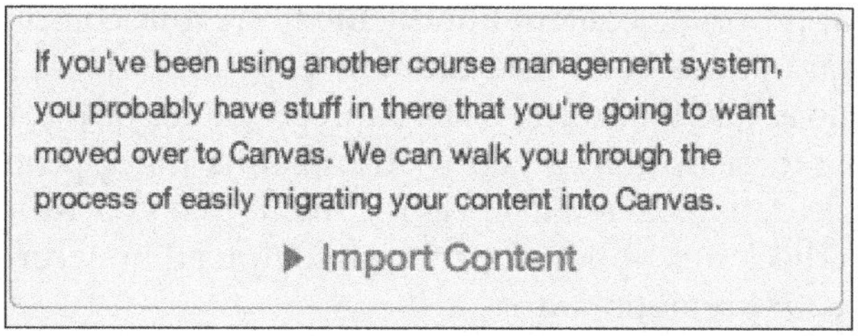

If you've been using another course management system, you probably have stuff in there that you're going to want moved over to Canvas. We can walk you through the process of easily migrating your content into Canvas.

▶ Import Content

3. On the page that appears, you will see the heading **Import Content** with a drop-down menu next to **Content Type**. From the drop-down menu, choose the type of content import you would like to import by selecting the file type and management system you have used in the past. For example, if you have an exported course from Blackboard or Moodle, choose the option that corresponds to the LMS with which you have created the course export file. The following screenshot displays the options you may choose from:

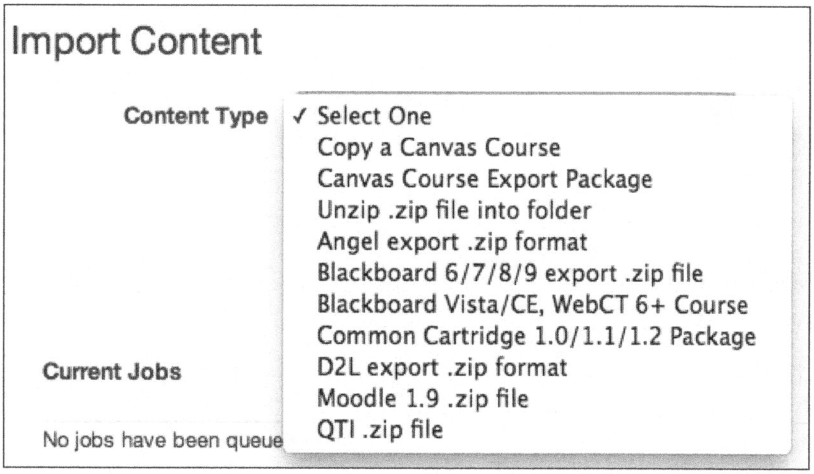

Import Content

Content Type
- ✓ Select One
- Copy a Canvas Course
- Canvas Course Export Package
- Unzip .zip file into folder
- Angel export .zip format
- Blackboard 6/7/8/9 export .zip file
- Blackboard Vista/CE, WebCT 6+ Course
- Common Cartridge 1.0/1.1/1.2 Package
- D2L export .zip format
- Moodle 1.9 .zip file
- QTI .zip file

Current Jobs

No jobs have been queue

4. After you have selected your content type, options will appear on the **Import Content** page that will guide you through uploading your content bundle.

5. Follow the instructions that appear for the type of content you are importing and check any relevant adjustment options. In most cases, you will see an option to upload the content bundle from your computer.

6. Select the appropriate content bundle file from your computer. You may see other appear options below the **Content Type** drop-down menu that include the ability to adjust the course's start and end dates or the assignment due dates. Select these options if you wish and enter the appropriate dates. You may also see options to select specific content that you would like to import to Canvas; check this option if you wish to upload only certain sections or files from your previous course.

7. Once you have selected the content bundle file to import and have selected the desired adjustment options, click on **Import**. From there, you will see your course import appear under **Current Jobs** at the bottom of the import screen.

8. You will see a progress bar appear, and once your import is finished, you will be able to see that the import is complete. You will also be able to see the time at which it was completed, as shown in the following screenshot:

Current Jobs			
Canvas Common Cartridge	...le-course-export.imscc	Oct 14 at 10:22am	Completed

9. When your import is completed, you can navigate back to the course's home page.

On the left-side menu, you can click through the navigation links to explore the content that has been imported. The **Assignments** or **Files** links on the left-side menu are the most common places for the imported content to appear, so feel free to click on those links to explore where your content has been imported.

The following sections will cover how to add to, adjust, modify, rearrange, or delete the content that you have now successfully imported.

Adding assignments and content

The bulk of building a course in Canvas is creating your assignments and setting up the grading preferences to accurately reflect the expectations in your syllabus. As we discussed, the more planning that goes into your course before you begin building it, the easier it will be for you to assemble your course. Once you have developed your syllabus, identify the assignments, assessments, and grading policies you would like to put into action for your course. When you have developed the graded content for your course in the abstract, you can begin building each assignment within your Canvas course.

Creating an assignment

The following section will walk you through creating assignments for your course. As we work through the options available to you as you create your assignments, you will gain a better understanding of the variety of purposes the assignments may serve within your course. To create your first assignment, perform the following steps:

1. Open the home page of your course.

2. On the left-side menu, click on **Assignments**. This will bring you to the assignment list for your course, which you will notice is empty (unless you have imported assignments from another course or LMS). Click on the plus sign icon to begin creating your first assignment, as seen in the following screenshot:

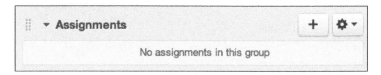

3. You will see a pop-up screen appear that includes options to designate the **Type**, **Name**, **Due**, and **Points** value for your first assignment. You will also see buttons to view **More Options**, the **Cancel** button to cancel the assignment creation, and the **Save** button to save (that is, create) the assignment.

4. For your first assignment, set the assignment type to **Assignment** for the purpose of learning the basics of assignment creation. We will discuss the four other types of assignments in the *Creating different types of assignments* section later in this chapter. Enter the name, due date, and point value for your assignment. When choosing the due date of your assignment, you can click on the small calendar icon next to the **Due** option, which will open a pop-up monthly calendar. Click on the day you would like to set as the due date, and then enter the time by which you would like the assignment to be turned in.

5. Click on **Save** to create your assignment. The following screenshot displays an example designated as **Assignment** named My First Assignment, due on September 19, 2014, and worth 100 points:

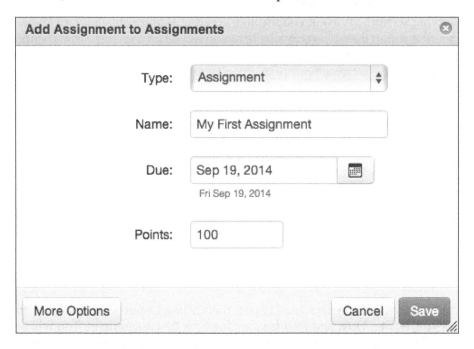

Your assignment name should reflect what your first assignment will be, for example, Week 1 Written Reflection or Getting-to-Know-You Video. The due date and points should correlate to your syllabus.

After you click on **Save**, you will have officially created your first assignment. This assignment will now show up in the course calendar and in the Gradebook with the due date and point value that you have assigned.

Editing an assignment

After you have created your basic assignment, you can click on the name of your newly created assignment, which will take you to the assignment page for that assignment. When creating future assignments, you can access this page by clicking on the **More Options** button instead of clicking on **Save** to create the assignment. You will see that the assignment page lists all of the specifications you entered when you created the assignment, but the page will not contain specific completion or submission instructions for that assignment (that is, **No content**). From here, we want to edit the assignment to add more specifics that will guide students to accurately complete and submit the assignment, whether they are submitting the assignment live or electronically. We also want to adjust the grading and assignment specifications to make sure that the grade we eventually enter into the **Gradebook** affects each student's overall grade accurately. To edit the assignment, click on the **Edit** button at the top-right corner of the assignment page, as shown in the following screenshot:

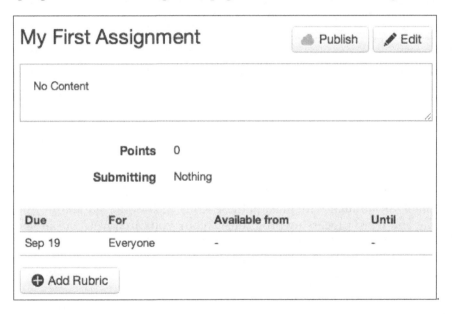

This will open the editing page for your first assignment. You will see the option to edit the name of the assignment at the top of the screen. Below that, you will find a Rich Content Editor that contains a menu bar full of formatting and content options above a textbox. Below the Rich Content Editor, you will see options for **Points**, **Assignment Group**, **Display Grade as**, **Submission Type**, **Group Assignment**, and **Peer Reviews** as well as the **Due Date** options at the very bottom. Before we delve into all of these features, let's start by familiarizing ourselves with the Rich Content Editor, which appears throughout Canvas as a way to customize posted content.

Using the Rich Content Editor

The Rich Content Editor allows you to post content to Canvas and customize the formatting for what you are posting. Formatting involves the presentation of the content (for example, the alignment, spacing, indentation, font color, and so on). The Rich Content Editor also allows you to do things such as insert a hyperlink, create a table, or upload media content (such as audio or video). If you hover your mouse over the icons in the Rich Content Editor, you will see a description of what each button does. Go ahead and hover your mouse to explore the options within the Rich Content Editor.

Basic formatting

The icons on the left-hand side and the drop-down menus on the right-hand side of the Rich Text Editor allow you to adjust the basic formatting of the text you wish to edit, as shown by the brackets in the following screenshot:

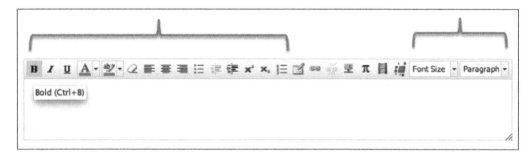

You will likely be familiar with most of these icons, as they are standard across many text editing and word processing programs. Again, you can hover your mouse over each icon to see a description of what each button will do. These basic formatting options adjust the appearance of the text within the textbox, for example, the size, emphasis, color, and position.

Embedding content

The icons indicated by the horizontal bracket in the following screenshot allow you to embed items into the textbox by navigating through the pop-up menus that appear when you click on each icon. The following sections describe each icon from left to right.

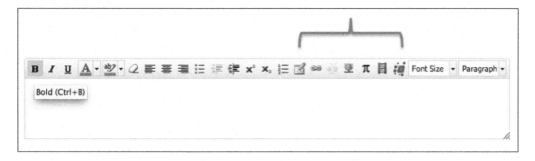

The Insert/Edit Table feature

The **Insert/Edit Table** feature allows you to insert a table, similar to a table you would generate using a spreadsheet program such as Microsoft Excel. To insert a table, perform the following steps:

1. Click on the **Insert/Edit Table** icon within the Rich Content Editor.

2. You will see a pop-up menu with two tabs at the top, the **General** tab and the **Advanced** tab, as shown in the following screenshot:

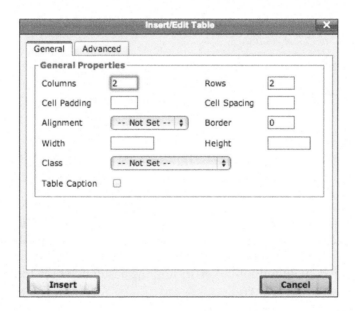

3. Based on the desired dimensions and characteristics of the table you wish to create, go through each option and type in the desired specifications. You will most likely only need to fill out the information under the **General** tab; however, feel free to explore the options available under the **Advanced** tab.

4. Once you have filled out everything to your liking, click on **Insert** in the bottom-left corner of the pop-up menu to create your table. If you are editing a table that you have already created, click on **Update** in the bottom-left corner of the pop-up menu.

The Link to URL feature

The **Link to URL** feature allows you to insert a hyperlink that will open a URL (that is, a website address) in a new tab or window in your web browser. The easiest way to insert a hyperlink is to copy and paste the link into the Rich Content Editor textbox, and it will automatically be converted into a link. Alternatively, you can click on the **Link to URL** icon to add a link or change plain text to a hyperlink. To create a hyperlink, perform the following steps:

1. Click on the **Link to URL** icon.

2. You will see a pop-up menu with instructions to paste a URL in the box shown in the pop-up window:

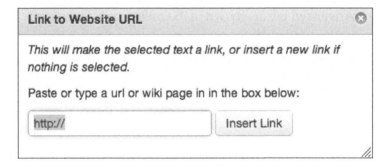

3. Once you have pasted the web address in the box, click on **Insert Link**. This will display the link you have pasted as a clickable hyperlink in the main textbox below the Rich Content Editor.

You can also highlight plain text and then click on the **Link to URL** icon to change the plain text to a hyperlink. In this case, the selected text will open the web address, but the full URL will not be displayed in the main text box. This allows you to embed links into written content without interrupting the aesthetic of the written content with a cumbersome web address.

If you paste the URL to a video hosted on YouTube, the Rich Content Editor will automatically embed a thumbnail of the video into the textbox. This allows users to click on the thumbnail and watch the video within the assignment or content page rather than opening a new tab or window in the web browser.

The Unlink feature

The **Unlink** feature allows you to remove a hyperlink that has been inserted using the **Link to URL** feature. To unlink a hyperlink, select the link and then click on the **Unlink** icon.

The Embed Image feature

The **Embed Image** feature allows you to embed an image into the textbox. When you click on the **Embed Image** icon, you will see a pop-up menu with three tabs at the top; the **URL**, **Canvas**, and **Flickr** tabs. Each of these tabs offers you a way to embed an image.

The **URL** tab allows you to paste the URL of an image that already exists online and embed the image. To add an image from a URL, perform the following steps:

1. Click on the **URL** tab and paste the URL for your image into the box at the top.

2. You may see an option to add alternative text for improved accessibility (optional) and adjust the dimensions of the image you wish to embed. Adjusting the dimensions basically allows you to resize the image so it does not fill the entire page once it is embedded. The aspect ratio (the proportional length and width of the image) will remain the same.

3. To embed the image, click on **Update** in the bottom-right corner of the pop-up window, as shown in the following screenshot:

The **Canvas** tab allows you to insert an image that has been uploaded to the **Files** section of your course. To add an image from Canvas, perform the following steps:

1. Click on the **Canvas** tab and locate the image within the **Files** section of your Canvas account.

2. If you have imported content from another system, you may have images that you have used for your course previously. These images will most likely appear in the **Files** section of your course, and you can select and adjust the dimensions of these images.

3. Click on the image to select it, then click on **Update**, as shown in the following screenshot:

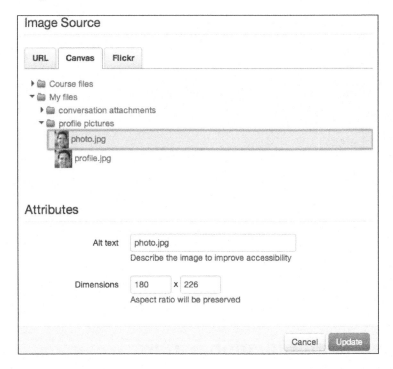

The **Flickr** tab allows you to search for Creative Commons images that are available for free use online. To find and embed images using the **Flickr** tab, perform the following steps:

1. Click on the **Flickr** tab and enter your search terms into the search bar.
2. Press *Enter* or click on the magnifying glass search icon.
3. Select the desired image from the search results that appear.

4. Enter the desired dimensions, and then click on **Update**, as shown in the following screenshot:

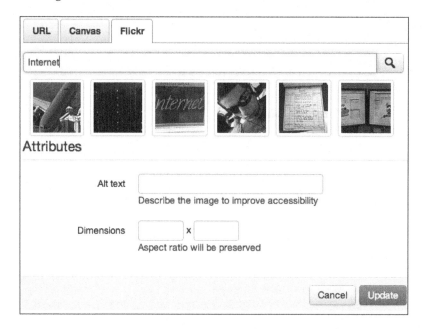

The Insert Math Equation feature

The **Insert Math Equation** feature allows you to insert a math equation into the textbox. To insert an equation, perform the following steps:

1. Click on the **Insert Math Equation** icon, which will open a pop-up menu with seven tabs. Each tab allows you to insert specific mathematical symbols to build basic or complex mathematical equations.

2. To insert a symbol, click on the desired symbol and make any necessary adjustments in the editing box below the symbols menu.

3. If you are familiar with the LaTeX code, you can click on **Switch View to Advanced** to enter or paste the LaTeX code.

4. When you have successfully created the desired math equation, click on **Insert Equation** in the bottom-right corner of the pop-up window, as shown in the following screenshot:

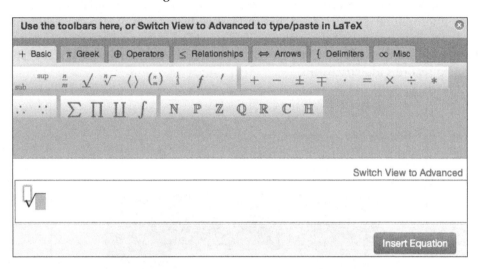

The Record/Upload Media feature

The **Record/Upload Media** feature allows you to record or upload audio and video and then embed that media into the textbox. When you click on the **Record/Upload Media** icon, you will see a pop-up menu with two tabs: the **Record Media** and **Upload Media** tabs. If you do not see a pop-up window appear, make sure your browser settings are adjusted to allow pop-ups from Canvas.

The Record Media tab

Within the **Record Media** tab, you will see a webcam icon and a microphone icon on the left-hand side of the **Title** box. To record and upload a video or audio, perform the following steps:

1. Click on the webcam icon to record and upload a video, or click on the microphone icon to record and upload audio. You may also see a dialogue box in the center of the pop-up window asking for access to your camera and/or microphone. Click on **Allow**, as shown in the following screenshot, to record video or audio:

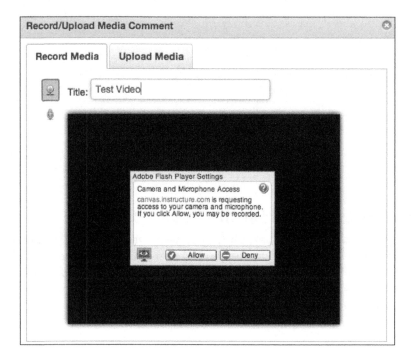

2. The webcam and/or microphone on your computer will turn on and you will see instructions that read **Click anywhere to start recording**, as shown in the following screenshot:

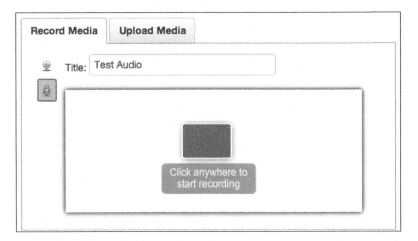

3. Once you click anywhere within the preview window, the video or audio recording will begin. The following screenshot shows you the instructions to start a video recording:

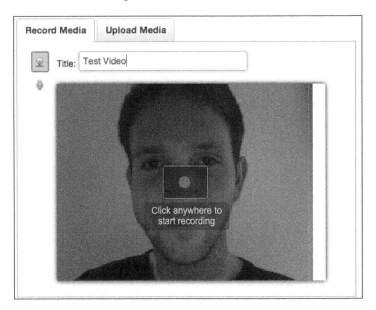

4. To end the recording, click anywhere within the preview window. You can rerecord the video/audio recording using the record icon that appears at the bottom of the preview window.

5. You can save and embed the recording by clicking on the **Save** option that appears at the bottom of the preview window.

If you have media on your computer that you would like to upload to your course, you can do so using the **Upload Media** tab.

The Upload Media tab

The **Upload Media** tab appears to the right of the **Record Media** tab within the pop-up window. To upload a video or audio to your course, perform the following steps:

To upload a video or audio to your course, perform the following steps:

1. Click on the **Upload Media** tab.

2. You will see two options **Select Audio File** and **Select Video File** to either select an audio file or select a video file, respectively. Make your selection, and then locate the file on your computer in the window that appears.

3. Once you have found the file, select it, and the upload will automatically begin, as shown in the following screenshot:

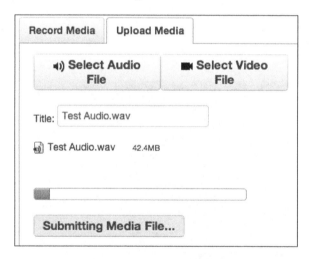

4. You will have the option to rename the file, which will appear in the **Files** section of your course once it has finished uploading. The finished upload will also appear embedded in the textbox of the Rich Content Editor.

Moving back to the features of the Rich Content Editor, let's discuss embedded services next.

Embedded services

In *Chapter 5*, *Exploring Special Features*, we will discuss the use of embedded services further. Once you have linked an embedded service to your Canvas account, these services will show up as icons in the Rich Text Editor. The following screenshot indicates the Equella embedded service, which gives you the option to embed links to content from the Equella online repository:

The HTML Editor feature

In addition to the wide variety of user-friendly formatting and embedding options available through the Rich Text Editor, Canvas also allows you to edit the HTML code directly. This allows users who are familiar with HTML code to manually adjust and modify the content of their pages. You can also paste HTML code to embed content from outside websites. To edit the HTML code, perform the following steps:

1. Click on the **HTML Editor** link in the upper-right corner of the Rich Text Editor, as shown in the following screenshot:

2. You will see any formatting or text you have inserted turn into HTML code that can be edited.

3. To return to the regular Rich Text Editor view, click on the **Visual Editor** link that now appears in the same place the HTML Editor link appeared previously.

Inserting content using the right-side menu

You will notice that whenever the Rich Content Editor is available to edit a Canvas page, the right-side menu of your course will allow you to insert even more content to enhance the capabilities of the Rich Content Editor. If you look at the right-side menu of your course, you will see three tabs that read **Links**, **Files**, and **Images**.

The Links tab

The **Links** tab allows you to create a hyperlink to content within your Canvas course. You will see a list of content within the course. While there is not much in your course at this point, once you have created assignments, wiki pages, or announcements, for example, you will be able to insert a link to those items by clicking on the item in the right-side menu. The following screenshot displays the **Links** tab:

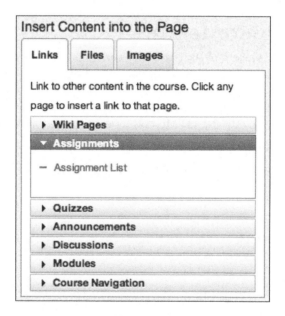

The Files tab

The **Files** tab allows you to quickly and easily upload files to your Canvas course and then link to those files directly. This is especially helpful if a certain file is necessary to complete an assignment, as students will have ready access to the file directly on the assignment page. Certain file types such as PDF documents will actually appear within the content page window, while other file types will be downloaded to students' computers when they click on the link. To add a new file to your course, perform the following steps:

1. Click on **Upload a new file**, and then select the file from your computer. You can choose a destination folder within your course, and then click on **Upload**.

2. Once your file is uploaded, it will appear within the designated folder and you can add a hyperlink to the file by clicking on the file name. A link to the file will appear in the textbox of the Rich Content Editor. The following screenshot displays the **Files** tab:

The Images tab

The **Images** tab functions very similarly to the **Embed Image** feature of the Rich Content Editor, except that the **Images** tab allows you to upload images from your computer to the course files. To add a new image, perform the following steps:

1. Click on **Upload a new image**, and then select the image file from your computer. You can choose a destination folder within your course, and then click on **Upload**.

2. Once your image is uploaded, it will appear within the **Images** tab. When your image appears in the **Images** tab, you can click on it to embed it in the textbox underneath the Rich Content Editor.

3. In addition to uploading your own images, you can also search for Creative Commons images on Flickr, just as with the **Embed Image** feature of the Rich Content Editor. The following screenshot displays the **Images** tab:

In addition to uploading files and images to your Canvas course using the right-side menu, you can manage your course files by clicking on the **Files** option on the left-side menu. There, you will be able to see all of the files that have been uploaded to your course and add folders to organize those files.

Editing an assignment – adding content

Now that we are familiar with the capabilities of the Rich Content Editor, which accompanies the right-side menu, we are ready to start adding content to our assignment. If you have closed the **Edit Assignment** screen, open up the assignment page and then click on **Edit**, just as we did previously. From there, you will see the same screen again with the Rich Content Editor and other adjustment options. Working from your syllabus, you can now begin to input instructions for your first assignment.

Type the assignment instructions into the textbox, and then add formatting using the icons on the left-hand side and far right-hand side of the Rich Content Editor. If you already have the instructions typed out in another document, you can also copy and paste them directly into the assignment page. The following points offer some suggestions for useful content that you may want to embed into your assignment page:

- Use the **Record/Upload Media** feature to record a video of yourself verbally explaining the instructions. You might consider doing this in addition to written instructions, or you might prefer to just record yourself giving instructions. Posting videos of yourself as the instructor can be very helpful for building a rapport with the students, especially in a fully online course where synchronous interaction might be limited.

- Use the **Link to URL** feature to embed a YouTube video. You might choose to embed a video as the content on which students will base their work for the assignment.

- Insert an image using the **Embed Image** feature to liven up the aesthetic of your assignment page. You could also insert images on which students could base their work for the assignment (for example, a political cartoon, artwork, and so on).

When you have finished inputting the content for your assignment page, you can make adjustments to the **Points** option for your assignment using the option underneath the textbox. For now, leave the **Assignment Group** option set to **Assignments**. We will discuss assignment groups in more detail at the end of this chapter. You can then adjust the other options listed in the following sections to customize your assignment.

The grading type

You can adjust what the grade for your assignment will look by clicking on the drop-down menu next to **Display Grade as**, as shown in the following screenshot:

Display Grade as	Percentage
	Complete/Incomplete
	✓ Points
	Letter Grade
	Not Graded

Click on one of the five drop-down items to select the type of grading you would like to utilize for the assignment. This feature is useful if you are required to submit final grades in a certain format. You can set your assignment preferences to allow you to grade assignments using different grading systems.

The Submission Type drop-down menu

Below the **Display Grade as** option, you can adjust the type of submission. This is a clear example of the flexibility of using Canvas for live or online courses, as the **Submission Type** drop-down menu clearly indicates options for **Online** or **On Paper** submissions. Also included are options for **No Submission** (such as attendance or participation grades) or **External Tool**, which we will cover in more detail in *Chapter 5*, *Exploring Special Features*. If you select the **Online** submission type, your screen will expand further to let you choose a variety of file types or submission formats, as shown in the following screenshot:

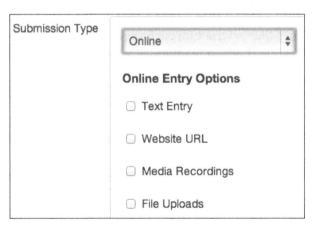

Depending on the kind of submission you are looking for, you may wish to limit the submission formats:

- **Text Entry**: This option will enable students to enter text directly, which might be a good option for assignments that require brief paragraph responses.

- **Website URL**: This option will enable students to paste a web address that you will be able to view when grading their submission. You might enable this feature if you require students to maintain an external blog or website for your class. This feature would allow them to submit the link to their work directly through Canvas.

- **Media Recordings**: This option will enable students to record and upload audio and video to submit for the assignment. You might enable this feature if you would like students to submit audio or video recordings of a presentation or performance, an edited video on the assigned topic, or speaking an essay response instead of typing it out.

- **File Uploads**: This option will enable students to submit a file (such as a word processing document, a spreadsheet, or a photo) for the assignment, which might be useful for research papers, budgets, or the documentation of a final project.

Group assignments

Below the **Submission Type** option, you will see the option to make the assignment a **Group Assignment**. If you click on the checkmark next to **This is a Group Assignment**, a pop-up window will appear that will allow you to create a set of groups for the assignment, specify how you would like to form the groups, and decide how you would like to structure each group. The following screenshot shows you the options available in the pop-up window:

Add Set of Groups	⊗

Name for Groups: | Project Groups

Self Sign-Up: ☐ Allow self sign-up ❓
☐ Require group members to be in the same section

Group Structure: ○ Split students into [ ] equal groups
◉ I'll create groups manually

[Create Category]

Once you have entered the details in the **Name for Groups** field, decided whether students can sign-up for groups using the **Self Sign-Up** option, and selected the **Group Structure**, you can click on **Create Category**. When the pop-up window is closed, you will see an **Assign Grades to Each Student Individually** checkbox that allows you to assign grades to each student individually. You can check this box if you would like to assign individual grades or leave it unchecked to assign the same grade to all students in a group. Once you have created a group category, you will be able to use the same specifications for other group assignments if you wish. For group assignments, you can also select from user groups that you might create when adding participants to your course, which we will cover in *Chapter 3, Getting Ready to Launch Your Course*.

Peer reviews

If you would like to require students to review their peers' work, you can check off the box next to **Require Peer Reviews**. When you check the peer review box, you will see the **Manually Assign Peer Reviews** or **Automatically Assign Peer Reviews** options. For manual peer reviews, you will receive a notification to assign a peer reviewer to each assignment as it is submitted. Alternatively, you can set up the assignment so Canvas automatically makes peer assignments at the time of submission.

Assignment availability

The final section of your new assignment allows you to select the availability of the assignment for the participants in your course. You can see the options of the final section in the following screenshot:

You can adjust whether the assignment is for everyone using Canvas or if it is only for students in your course. You can adjust the **Due Date** value, and you can set the length of time the assignment will be available to participants. Setting the availability limits when participants have access to the assignment page and restricts when students can make a submission to the assignment page. For example, you may wish to only allow students to view an introductory assignment page and make a submission during the first two weeks of your course, so you could set the availability to limit the time frame during which students could interact with the assignment page.

Updating and publishing an assignment

When you have finished adding content and adjusting the settings for your assignment, you are ready to update and publish the assignment. To update and publish your assignment, perform the following steps:

1. When you finish editing your assignment, click on the **Update Assignment** button at the bottom of the page, and you will be taken back to the assignment page.

2. At the top-right corner of the assignment page, click on the **Publish** button, as shown in the following screenshot next to the **Edit** button. You will notice that the button changes color from gray to green when you publish the assignment.

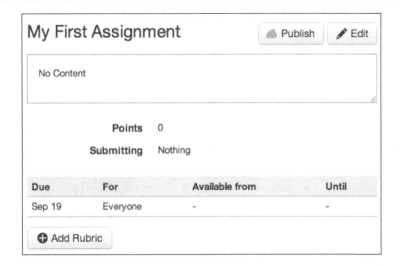

 If you are editing an assignment after you have published your course, you can check the box at the bottom of the **Edit Assignment** page that reads **Notify users that this content has changed**. This triggers a notification to all users involved with the course that you have edited and updated the assignment.

Creating different types of assignments

Now that you have successfully created your first assignment (remember, we designated the type of the first assignment as an **Assignment**), we can explore the four other types of assignments that you can create using Canvas. The different types of assignments can serve as assessment tools for you and can offer a variety of activities for students to complete. Just as in a live course, students might encounter quizzes, tests, essays, projects, presentations, or debates in your Canvas course. The designated assignment types can accommodate each of these traditional assignment styles in a variety of ways. You are welcome to adapt the designated assignment type to fit your needs.

To create the different types of assignments, navigate back to the assignment list for your course by clicking on **Assignments** on the left-side menu. You will see an assignment group with your first assignment listed below the assignment group heading. To create a new assignment of a different type, perform the following steps:

1. Click on the plus sign icon that appears to the right of the assignment group bar:

2. Once you have begun to create your new assignment, click on the drop-down menu next to **Type** as you are creating your assignment. You will see the following options:

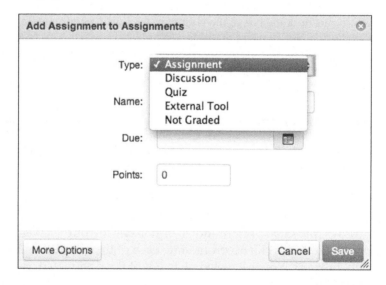

From the options that appear, you may choose to use any of the assignment type options. Some people choose to use all five types for different assignments in their course, while some people choose to only use one type. It all depends on your how you would like students to interact with the assignment and how you would like to collect, assess, and grade the work. To gain a better understanding of how to use each assignment type, let's take a look at each type individually.

Assignment

The first assignment we created was designated as an **Assignment**. This designation can accommodate tasks wherein students submit a piece of work to you for assessment and grading. You have great flexibility with the assignment design and submission options, as detailed in the previous section. Once students have submitted their assignment, you will be able to see their work and offer them feedback. The work submitted for an **Assignment** can only be viewed by the student who has submitted the assignment and you; grades always remain private.

Discussion

A **Discussion** assignment creates a graded discussion thread in your course wherein students submit written comments or links in reply to a posted topic. Everyone in the course can see and comment on the discussion topics. When students post something on the discussion board, their post appears as their submission for the assignment, which you can then view and grade. As the content posted in discussions is viewable by everyone in the course, **Discussion** assignments can be a valuable tool for cooperative learning and peer review. Though the posts are public within the course, students' grades remain private.

After you create a **Discussion** assignment, you will be able to edit the discussion by clicking on the assignment name, which will open up the course discussion board to the discussion assignment that you have created. You can also access the course discussion board by clicking on the **Discussions** link on the left-side menu. To edit the discussion topic, perform the following steps:

1. Click on **Edit** in the top-right corner of the discussion page, as shown in the following screenshot:

2. When you click on **Edit**, you will see a screen with the Rich Content Editor and assignment options below the Rich Content Editor textbox. Hopefully, this type of screen is starting to look familiar! Enter the content for your discussion topic.

3. Below the textbox, you will see options that are similar to the ones we edited for our first assignment. Some of the options look slightly different for **Discussion** assignments:

   ° **Attachment**: This feature allows you to attach a file to your discussion topic post, which students can download and use for their responses. To use this feature, click on **Choose File** and then locate the file that you would like to attach from your computer. Once you have selected the file, click on **Open** in the pop-up window, and the file will be attached once you update the discussion post.

   ° **Allow threaded replies**: This feature allows students to comment on other students' posts within a discussion thread. Allowing threaded replies will enable students to keep the conversation going rather than simply posting one response to the original topic.

   ° **Users must post before seeing replies**: This feature allows the posts in a graded discussion assignment to remain hidden from individual students until each of them has posted a response. You might consider using this feature to encourage originality in students' responses rather than letting students wait to post a response until they see what other students have already posted.

   ° **Enable podcast feed**: This feature allows you to let students subscribe to the discussion thread as a podcast, so they will see updates to the discussion thread along with their other podcast updates. If you select **Enable podcast feed**, you will see another option, **Include Replies in podcast feed**, which will allow students to see the discussion topic and the posted replies in their podcast feeds. If you enable the podcast feed option, you will see a link to the podcast feed appear on the list of course discussions. Once the course is published, students will be able to click on that link and view the podcast feed for that discussion.

   ° **Graded**: Because you created the discussion as an assignment, this box will be checked. Checking this box allows you to give students a grade for their contribution to the discussion.

4. Below these options, you will see the same advanced options that we discussed when setting up our first assignment.

5. Once you have finished updating the content and settings for your discussion assignment, you can click on **Save** at the bottom of the page.

6. When you have saved your changes, click on the **Publish** button in the top-right corner of the discussion page next to the **Edit** button.

Once you have created and published your discussion, you may choose to pin the discussion to the top of the discussion board or close a discussion for comments. Pinning a discussion organizes the discussion board so your students will see **Pinned Discussions** listed first whenever they view the discussion board. Closing a discussion for comments prevents students from contributing to discussions that are **Closed for Comments**.

To pin a discussion or close a discussion for comments, perform the following steps:

1. Click on the **Discussions** tab on the left-side menu of your course.

2. Find the discussion you would like to pin or close for comments, and then click-and-drag that discussion into the **Pinned Discussions** section at the top of the discussion board or the **Closed for Comments** section at the bottom of the discussion board.

3. You can also pin or close a discussion by clicking on the gear icon to the right of the discussion title on the discussion board. Select **Pin** or **Close for comments** from the drop-down list, as shown in the following screenshot:

As your course progresses, you and your students may create numerous discussion threads. Pinning discussions or closing them for comments allows you to organize and keep track of discussions within your course based on their importance.

Quiz

A **Quiz** assignment allows you to create a quiz within your Canvas course that students can complete online. You are able to design the questions and incorporate a number of traditional question types while setting the various parameters for taking the quiz (for example, the time constraints).

To create a quiz, perform the following steps:

1. Return to the assignment list by clicking on **Assignments** on the left-side menu.

2. Click on the plus sign icon on the assignment group bar, and then select **Quiz** from the **Type** drop-down menu.

3. Once you save the new quiz assignment, click on the title to view the quiz page. You can also access the quiz by clicking on **Quizzes** on the left-side menu of your course.

4. At the top of that page, you will see a message that notifies you that the quiz is unpublished and that only teachers can see the quiz before it is published. You will need to publish each quiz that you create individually once you have finished building the quiz.

5. To build the quiz question by question, click on **Edit** on the quiz page just underneath the message.

Editing the settings for your quiz

When the quiz-editing page is opened, you should recognize the Rich Text Editor and the options below it. It is important to notice that there are two tabs at the top of the quiz editing page, the **Settings** tab and the **Questions** tab, as shown in the following screenshot. It is easiest to begin on the **Settings** page by putting in the general instructions for the entire quiz and adjusting the settings listed below the textbox as you see fit:

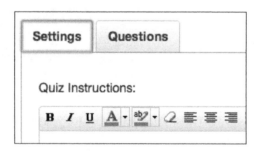

Under the textbox, you will see a drop-down menu for **Quiz Type**; if you click on this drop-down, you are given the option to make the quiz a **Practice Quiz**, a **Graded Quiz**, a **Graded Survey**, or an **Ungraded Survey**. Quizzes serve to assess students' learning as students answer content-related questions, while surveys serve to collect information from students. You can choose which type of quiz you would like to create, and then move down the list of settings for your quiz. We will discuss grouping assignments a little later on, so for now, continue to the following list of settings:

- **Shuffle Answers**: This option allows you to alternate the order of the answers when the same question is displayed on different computers, or if you allow students to take the quiz multiple times.

- **Time Limit**: This option allows you to restrict the amount of time students have to complete the quiz once they begin.

- **Allow Multiple Attempts**: This option enables students to take the quiz more than once. When you check this box, you will see options that allow you to designate which score to keep as the student's grade and how many times students are allowed to retake the quiz.

- **Let Students See Their Quiz Responses**: This option will show students their answers after they answer each question. If you check this option, another option appears that allows you to choose whether to display the correct answer to students once they have answered a question.

- **Show one question at a time**: This option requires students to move through the quiz sequentially rather than seeing the entire quiz and answering questions out of order. Through this option, you can also lock questions after answering them to prevent students from changing their answers.

- **Quiz Restrictions**: This option allows you to control who has access to the quiz. With this option, you can assign and require an access code to take the quiz, which basically acts like a password for students to access the quiz. In addition, you can filter who can take the quiz based on the range of their IP address. You may use this setting to limit students to only taking the quiz within a computer lab at your institution or within the wireless network of your institution.

The availability and date settings are the same as the other types of assignments we have talked about, so you can adjust them as required and then move on to adding questions and question groups to your quiz.

Adding questions to your quiz

Once you have input the general instructions for the quiz and adjusted all of the quiz settings as required, you can click on the **Questions** tab above the Rich Text Editor. This will present you with the three different options as displayed in the following screenshot:

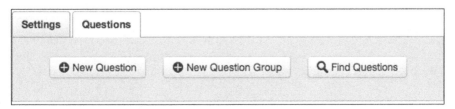

As you are creating your first quiz, you will need to create all of your quiz questions individually. To add a new question, perform the following steps:

1. Click on the **New Question** button, which will open a new blank question template.

2. The default question type is **Multiple Choice**, but you can choose from a large number of question types by clicking on the drop-down menu at the top of the **New Question** page, as shown in the following screenshot:

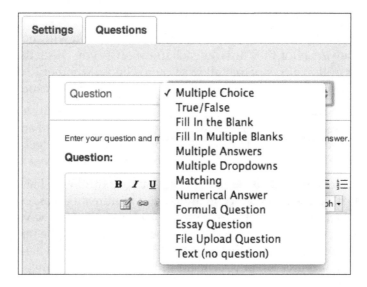

3. Once you select the question type, type the question into the textbox of the Rich Content Editor. Instructions on how to format the questions appear above the Rich Content Editor.

4. The answer options below the Rich Content Editor will change to reflect the specific parameters of the selected question type. Fill in the answer or possible answers in the area below the Rich Content Editor. The following screenshot offers an example of a **Fill In the Blank** question. Notice the instructions above the Rich Content Editor as well as the possible answers below it:

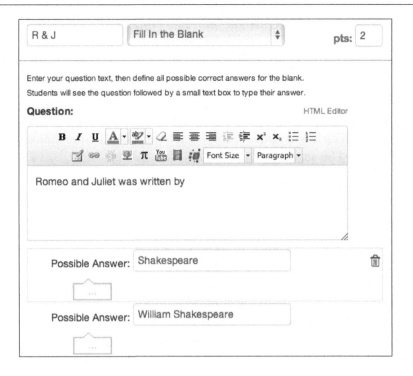

5. If you would like to add additional possible answers, click on the **Add Another Answer** button. You can also add comments that will appear when students answer the question. You may add comments for the correct answers by clicking on the green comment box, incorrect answers by clicking on the red box, and general comments for all answers by clicking on the blue box. The following screenshot shows each of these options:

6. After you have finished creating all of your quiz questions, click on the **Update Question** button in the bottom corner.

Once you have begun adding questions, the **New Question Group** button will allow you to arrange the questions into categories and groups. From there, you can allow students to choose how many questions from the group they would like to answer and how many points each question will be worth. You also have the **Link to a Question Bank** option to link to a question bank.

You will be able to create and manage question banks by clicking on the **Find Questions** button, which will allow you to search for and add questions that you have already created for other quizzes.

To find and add previously created questions to your quiz, perform the following steps:

1. Click on the **Find Questions** button. A screen appears, listing all of the questions you have created for the current quiz. If you have created other quizzes, you will see those questions appear as well.

2. Select the questions you wish to add by clicking on the checkbox next to each question. You can click on the **Select All** button to select all of the questions listed or click on **Clear All** to clear your selections.

3. Scroll down and click on the **Add Questions** button at the bottom of the pop-up window to add the selected questions to your quiz.

Managing question banks

The **Find Questions** pop-up window also includes the **Manage Course Question Banks** option to manage your course question banks. Question banks allow you to organize and arrange your questions for use across multiple quizzes. To create or edit question banks, perform the following steps:

1. Click on the **Find Questions** button.

2. In the top-right corner of the pop-up window, click on **Manage Course Question Banks**, as displayed in the following screenshot:

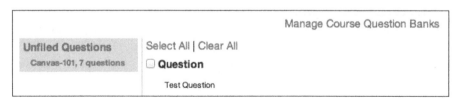

3. On the page that opens, you can create a new question bank by clicking on the **Add Question Bank** button on the right-side menu of the page. You can then type in the information for the new question bank on the template that appears in the center of your screen:

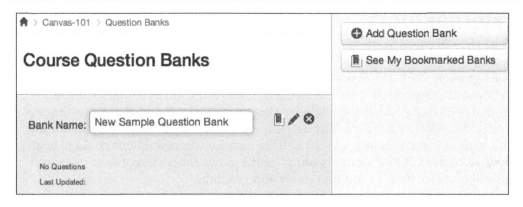

4. After you have typed in the title of the new bank, press *Enter* or *Return* on your keyboard to create the question bank.

5. Once you have created a new question bank, you can click on the title to open the question bank. The options pictured in the following screenshot appear on the right-side menu and allow you to edit and adjust the question bank to your liking:

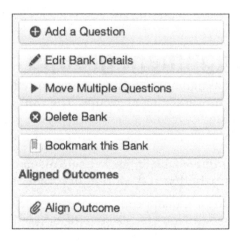

6. Once you are satisfied with your new or edited question bank, you can return to your quiz by clicking on the **Quizzes** tab on the left-side menu of your course.

Once your quiz is saved, you will be redirected back to the quiz page, where the message that notifies you that the quiz is unpublished will appear again at the top. When your quiz is completely built, you must publish your quiz by clicking on the **Publish** button before students will be able to take it.

External tools

While we will cover the details of enabling external tools in *Chapter 5, Exploring Special Features*, let's discuss what an external tool is and what it might look like as an assignment. Canvas has partnered with a large number of online resources to allow you to integrate their services directly into your Canvas course. The list of external tools that you have available to you varies based on what your institution has decided to make available through Canvas. An example of an assignment that utilizes an external tool might be an outside website where students could play an educational game. Once students complete the game, that external website would report their score back to you for review and grading.

Not Graded

You may choose to create assignments that are not graded, just as you would make assignments in a live class each day. These types of assignments might include bringing certain materials to class on a given day, handing in homework, or being present for a synchronous online meeting. **Not Graded** assignments most often serve to place heavy emphasis on certain information you would like your students to know, either at a specific time or throughout the duration of the course.

Creating assignment groups

As you work to create the assignments from your course syllabus, you may want to organize the assignments into assignment groups. You can create new assignment groups, adjust their weighted percentage, and add specific grading rules for each assignment group. To create an assignment group, perform the following steps:

1. Click on the **Assignments** tab on the left-side menu of your course, then click on the **+ Group** button at the top-right corner of the assignments page.

2. In the pop-up window that appears, you can type in **Group Name** for the new assignment group. You will also see the option to adjust % **of total grade**, but you will not be able to adjust this option until you change the assignment weight settings for your course, which we will discuss in the next section, *Weighting assignment groups*.

3. After you have entered **Group Name**, click on the **Save** button.

4. From there, drag the assignments that you have already created into your new assignment group. To move an existing assignment to a different assignment group, click on the dots that appear to the left-hand side of the assignment name, and then drag the assignment underneath the desired assignment group heading, as shown in the following screenshot:

Once you have created your assignment groups and dragged your assignments into the correct groups, you can specify grading rules for each group. To specify grading rules for an assignment group, perform the following steps:

1. Click on the gear icon to the right-hand side of the assignment group name and select **Edit** from the drop-down menu.

2. The pop-up menu that appears includes the same options that you saw when you created the assignment group with the added ability to designate **Number of scores to ignore for each student**. You may choose to automatically drop the highest or lowest score of any assignment within an assignment group. You can also choose to never drop the score of certain assignments. The example in the following screenshot indicates that only the lowest score within the assignment group would be dropped, and the score for Sample Quiz would never be dropped even if it was the lowest score within the assignment group:

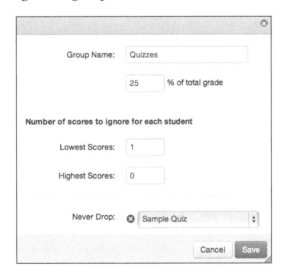

3. When you have finished creating the grading rules for your new assignment group, click on **Save** at the bottom-right corner of the pop-up window.

Weighting assignment groups

Creating assignment groups not only organizes the assignments to let students see what they will need to complete for your course, but it also gives you the option to weight groups of assignments. In many traditional grading systems, certain types of assignments may count for various percentages of a student's final grade. For example, homework might make up 20 percent, quizzes might make up 30 percent, essays might make up 35 percent, and the final project might make up 15 percent. By creating assignment groups, you can quickly and easily arrange the assignments you have already created. This way, Canvas will be set up to automatically calculate their final grade as you grade their work throughout the duration of your course. To weight assignment groups, perform the following steps:

1. Navigate to the course assignments page by clicking on the **Assignments** option on the left-side menu of your course.

2. You will see the assignment groups that house all of the assignments you have created thus far. To weight the assignment groups, click on the edit icon that looks like a gear at the top-right corner of the **Assignments** page. This icon is located to the right of the **+Group** and **+Assignment** buttons.

3. Within the window that pops up, check the box that reads **Weight final grade based on assignment groups**.

4. When you check that box, notice that the assignment groups appear below the checkbox with a table of assignment group weights. You can then set each assignment group to make up a customized percentage of the final grade, as shown in the following screenshot:

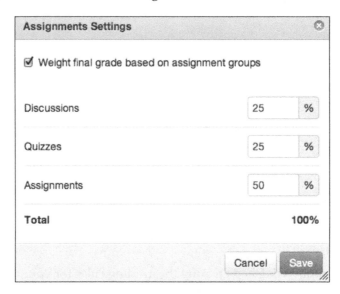

After you have organized all of your assignments into the desired groups, look back over the table of assignment group weights next to each assignment group. You can edit your assignment groups by editing each individual group, or you can click on the edit icon in the top-right corner of the **Assignments** page to edit all of the group weights at once.

If you decide that you would rather not weight students' final grades based on the assignment groups, all you need to do is uncheck the weighting option after clicking on the edit icon at the top-right corner of the **Assignments** page.

Summary

We started this chapter with a discussion of the **Next Steps** checklist that appears when you open the home page of your new course for the first time. We next moved on to planning your course, and then we worked through how to import content from another course. Next, we dove into adding assignments and content and became acquainted with the Rich Content Editor. After this, we adjusted the basic and advanced assignment settings and then discussed creating different types of assignments. Finally, we explored how to create assignment groups and how to weight grades based on the assignment groups.

After having covered many of the skills that you need in order to add more content to your course, we will continue through the **Next Steps** checklist in *Chapter 3, Getting Ready to Launch Your Course*. We will focus on the organization and presentation of your course, and then we will move on to adding students to the course and preparing your course to be published.

3
Getting Ready to Launch Your Course

In the previous chapter, we created the assignments for your course. Now, we can proceed through the rest of the checklist that appears on the home page of your course. In this chapter, we will cover the following topics:

- Adding participants to your course so they can access content
- Selecting navigation links for the left-side menu that will be most useful to your students during the course
- Choosing a course home page layout
- Adding the course's calendar events
- Publishing your course

By the end of this chapter, you will have your course totally built, organized, designed, and published in order to begin using Canvas to teach your course in *Chapter 4*, *Teaching Your Canvas Course*. Let's begin by adding students to the course.

Adding participants to the course

This section deals with manually adding participants to your course, which you may or may not have to do depending on the way your institution has integrated Canvas with its registration systems and technology departments. If your institution has integrated Canvas with its registration system, students and other participants may automatically be placed into your course upon its initial creation. However, if you have manually created the course or if your institution does not automatically create courses and add participants for you, you will need to follow the guidelines in this section to add people to your course.

Now that the content of your course is created, we can add participants to the course. As we work our way through the process of adding participants to your course, keep in mind that students and observers will not receive anything from you via Canvas until you have published the course. Other types of participants, which we will discuss shortly, may or may not be able to see the course before it is published, depending on the role you assign them within the course. By adding students to the course at this point, you are simply placing their contact information in a queue, which Canvas will use to send out e-mail invitations for the course once you have completed the course design and published it. You can think of this stage of building your course simply as creating your roster before you actually meet your students. There are two main ways to go about adding students to your course, which are as follows:

1. For the first option, navigate to the home page for your course, then look at the **Course Setup Checklist** that appears at the bottom of your screen. Remember, if you don't see the checklist, click on the **Course Setup Checklist** button at the top of the right-side menu. The third option on the checklist will be **Add Students to the Course**, which is shown in the following screenshot. When you click on that option, you will be taken to the **People** page for the course, where you will be able to add students.

2. Another option is to click directly on the **People** tab on the left-side menu of your course.

3. Once you are on the **People** page for your course, you will see a list of individuals who have already participated in your course. At this point, you will most likely only see yourself listed, unless your institution has automatically added your students for you.

Name	Login / SIS ID	Section	Role
Ryan John	youremail@sample.com	Canvas LMS Course Design	Teacher

4. Above the list of participants, you will see a search bar to search for individuals, a drop-down menu to limit the types of individuals you would like to view, and a button to add people. Click on the **Add People** button, and you will see a pop-up window with a text box where you can paste the e-mail addresses of the students you would like to add.

5. If you would like to include students' first and last names when you add them to the course, you have three options as demonstrated by the grayed-out text in the pop-up window. As you enter participants' contact information, separate all entries with commas. The following bullet points and the screenshot that follows them offer examples of how you can add students' information:

   ° Enter a student's first and last name within quotation marks, and then enter their e-mail address in brackets. For example:

   "Ryan John" <ryanjohn@example.com>,

   ° Enter a student's last name with a comma, and then enter their first name, all within quotation marks followed by their e-mail address in brackets. For example:

   "John, Ryan" <ryanjohn@example.com>,

○ Enter a student's e-mail address and separate entries with commas. For this option, students' names will show up within the course as their email address until they configure their own individual Canvas settings to display their name. For example, ryanjohn@example.com:

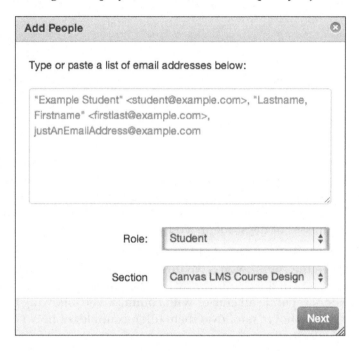

6. Once you have entered all of the e-mail addresses for people you wish to add to the course, you can select what type of users they will be once they are added to the course. The drop-down menu below the text box will allow you to add people to the course as a student, a teacher, a TA (Teacher's Assistant), a designer, or an observer. Each of these distinctions will allow participants to function within their designated role for the duration of the course. These distinctions allow participants to see and do different things within your course, either before or after the course is published:

○ **Students**: Participants added to the course as **Students** will not be able to see the course content until the course is published. Once you publish the course, they will be able to see all of the course content you have made available to them, and they will be able to submit assignments. They will have a line within the *Gradebook* (to be discussed in *Chapter 4, Teaching Your Canvas Course*). In general, students cannot edit the course content unless you alter the settings to allow them to do so.

- ○ **Teachers**: Participants added to the course as **Teachers** have all of the same abilities that you do within your course and are able to see the course before and after it is published. They can add and change the course content, adjust settings, add or remove users, and grade assignments.

- ○ **TAs**: Participants added to the course as teacher's assistants, referred to within Canvas as **TAs**, are largely able to see and do the same things as teachers within the course, but with the distinction of being the TA for the course. They can add and change the course content, adjust settings, add or remove users, and grade assignments. There are, however, a few things that TAs cannot do, such as publishing the course.

- ○ **Designers**: Participants added to the course as **Designers** are able to see the course before it is published. In most cases, someone would be added as a **Designer** to build the course for you, so they are able to add and change the course content, adjust settings, and organize the course. They are not able to see the assignment submissions or grade students' work.

- ○ **Observers**: Participants added to the course as **Observers** are not able to see the course until it is published. Observers have most of the same privileges as students, except that they cannot submit assignments, and they do not receive a line in the *Gradebook*. You can link observers to specific students, and the observer will be able to see the work of a specific student. An example of when you might add someone to the course as an observer might be of an administrator or parent who wants to see how a student is doing in a course, or a prospective student who wants to see what life in an online course at your institution is like.

7. You should add participants to your course in groups or as individuals, based on their role within your course. As such, it would make sense to add all of your students at one time or all of your observers at one time. You can certainly add people individually, as will probably be the case when you add any TAs or Designers to your course.

8. Once you have added the contact information and designated the role that the new participants will fulfill in the course, you can click on **Next** at the bottom of the pop-up window.

9. Once you click on **Next**, you should see a message that informs you that the e-mail addresses you entered have been validated and you are now ready to add those users to the course.

10. Double-check to make sure that everyone you intended to add to the course is on the list of validated participants, and then click on the **Add Users** button at the bottom right of the pop-up window, as shown in the following screenshot:

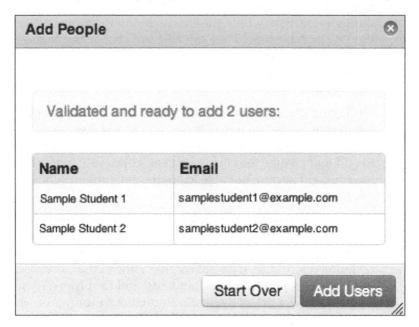

11. When you have clicked on **Add Users**, the pop-up window will close and you will see the list of new participants appear on the **People** page of your course. You will notice a bubble that reads **Pending** next to all of the new participants' names. Students and observers will not receive an invitation to join the course until you have published it. However, teachers, TAs, and designers will receive an e-mail invitation after you click on **Add Users**. Their status in the course will remain **Pending** until they follow the link in the e-mail to accept their invitation to the course. Once someone has accepted their invitation to join the course, you will see their name on the **People** page without the **Pending** status.

Managing users

You may find that you need to resend an invitation, edit the sections a participant is involved with, view the details of an individual's participation, or remove a user from the course. To accomplish any of these tasks, complete the following steps:

1. Click on the **People** button on the left-side menu of your course.

2. If you hover your mouse over any participant's name, you will see a gear icon appear on the right-hand side, next to their role designation. Click on the gear icon to manage the desired user, and you will see the following menu appear:

3. When you click on **Resend Invitation**, **Edit Sections**, or **Remove from Course**, you will see an instructional pop-up window appear that allows you to accomplish the desired task.

4. If you would like to know more about a specific user, click on **User Details** to see information about and adjust settings for individual users. You will be taken to the participant's details page, where you can view their course memberships, manage their privileges, and see their login information.

If you add a participant as an **Observer**, they will be able to see the public course content such as assignment pages or discussions, but will not be able to see any private content such as assignment submissions or grades. In some situations, you may be adding a participant as an observer to monitor a specific student, for example, a parent, administrator, or a tutor. You can link an observer to a specific student, which will allow the observer to see the student's grades and interactions within the course. To link an observer to a student, complete the following steps:

1. Click on the **People** button on the left-side menu of your course.

2. Find the observer you wish to link to a student and hover your mouse over their name. Click on the gear icon that appears to the right of their information, then click on **Link to Students** from the drop-down menu that appears, as shown in the following screenshot:

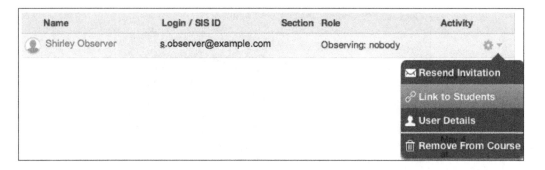

3. In the pop-up window that appears, type the name of the student with whom you wish to link the observer, and click on the student's name when it appears below the search bar. The pop-up window is shown in the following screenshot:

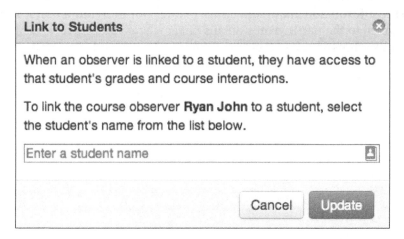

4. Once you have selected the student that the observer will be linked to, click on **Update**. The observer will now be able to see the student's interactions in the course as well as their assignment submissions and grades. You can remove or adjust the observer's student link by following the preceding steps and changing the student selection in the pop-up window.

Now that you have added users and learned how to manage their roles, let's talk about how you can organize your users into groups if you are planning to incorporate group assignments and collaborations into your course.

Creating user groups

As you are adding users, you may wish to create user groups that organize participants and provide space within the course for collaboration between participants who are grouped together. Creating user groups also makes it easy to select groups for group assignments or to message groups of users all at once. This option is not mandatory, so you may skip ahead to the next section if you do not plan on organizing users into groups at any point during your course. To create user groups, complete the following steps:

1. Click on the **People** link on the left-side menu of your course.

2. On the **People** page, click on the **View User Groups** button that appears on the right-side menu.

3. The page that appears explains what you can do after creating student user groups. Read the explanation, and then click on the **+ Group Set** button above the instructions, as shown in the following screenshot. You must first create a group set, and then you can create specific user groups within the group set.

Student Groups

+ Group Set

Student groups are a useful way to organize students for things like group projects or papers. Every student group gets their own calendar, discussion board and collaboration tools so they can organize themselves and work together more effectively.

You can randomly assign students to groups of a specific size, or manually create and organize the groups. Once your groups are created, you can set assignments to be "group submission" assignments, which means each group will have one submission for all users of that group.

4. A pop-up window that allows you to designate the **Group Set Name**, **Self Sign-Up** permission, and **Group Structure** will appear. When deciding on these preferences, think about the way user groups will function within your course. You may choose to create a group set that you can utilize for a specific group assignment, or you may choose to have certain students work with each other for the entire duration of your course:

   ° For the **Group Set Name**, choose a name that describes how the user groups will be used. For example, if you will use the groups for a group assignment, consider including the assignment name in the **Group Set Name**.

   ° If you would like to allow students to sign up for their groups themselves, check the box next to **Allow self sign-up**. Notice that the options for the **Group Structure** change if you allow self sign-up.

   ° In determining the **Group Structure**, you can have Canvas automatically split students into a certain number of groups, or you can create the groups manually after you have created the group set. If you are allowing self sign-up, you can designate the number of groups within the set as well as how many students can join each group.

5. Click on **Save** to create your new group set.

If you elected for Canvas to automatically split students into groups, this will happen now and you will see the groups once the pop-up window closes. If you elected to create groups manually, you will see a list of unassigned students and an empty group set. To manually create groups within the group set, complete the following steps:

1. Click on the gray **+ Group** button in the top-right corner, as shown in the following screenshot:

2. In the pop-up window that appears, enter **Group Name** and then click on **Save**.

3. To add students to the group, find a student you would like to add to the group from the list of unassigned students. To add them to the group, you can click on the dots next to the student's name, and drag them into the group. You can also click the **+** symbol next to the student's name and select the group from the drop-down menu that appears, as shown in the following screenshot:

4. You can continue to add users to the group in the same manner and then create new user groups within the set depending on your needs.

Now that you have added users and explored how to manage participants within your course, let's move on to organizing the presentation of your course by changing the navigation links that participants will see on the left-side menu of your course.

Selecting navigation links

The next step in the course setup checklist found on the home page of your course is learning how to select navigation links. The navigation links appear on the left-side menu of your course, and you can decide which of these links your students see when they log in to participate:

1. You can find where to change the navigation links in two ways:
   - Click on **Select Navigation Links** in the course setup checklist on your course home page.
   - Click on **Settings** at the bottom of the left-side menu of your course, and then click on the **Navigation** tab at the top of the **Settings** page.

2. When you have reached the **Navigation** tab of the **Settings** page, you will see a list of the available navigation links that you have the option to display for your course. You can reorder the links by clicking-and-dragging them, or you can disable and hide certain links from students to simplify the options by dragging the links to the bottom half of the screen. The following example has about half of the links hidden or disabled to simplify the presentation of the course:

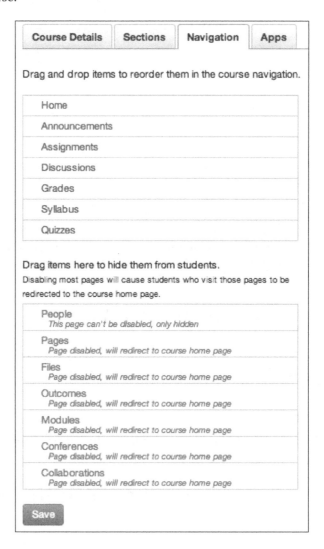

3. When you have finished arranging the navigation links and have decided which links you would like students to see, click on the **Save** button at the bottom of the screen.

Once you have saved your preferences, you will notice that you can still see all of the navigation links on the left-side menu, but the links that your students will be able to see appear in black and the links you have hidden or disabled appear in gray.

When deciding on which links to display to your students and which links to hide, consider what types of content you have made available to your students and the ways in which you have organized your course. For example, if you have decided against using the discussion feature of Canvas altogether and have not created any discussion posts or discussion assignments, you might consider hiding the discussion navigation link to simplify where students can go while exploring your course. In keeping with the idea of simplifying and streamlining, let's move on to the next part of the course setup checklist, which is choosing a home page layout.

Choosing a course home page layout

The home page for your course is the first thing your students will see when they log in. Even the most well-prepared courses can stall at the beginning if the directions for accessing the course content are not clear; therefore, choosing the best home page layout for your course is an important task. To accommodate a variety of needs and teaching styles, Canvas has made it possible to choose from five different course home page layouts. To select from these options, complete the following steps:

1. Go to the home page of your course, and then click on the **Edit Homepage** link in the right-side menu, as shown in the following screenshot:

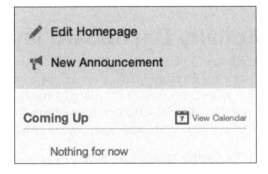

2. After you click on the **Edit Homepage** link, you will see a pop-up window with a drop-down menu from which you can choose one of the five layouts. The following screenshot shows you the five options that appear in the drop-down menu:

3. Select one of the layouts, and then click on the **Save** button to update your course home page.

Let's now take a look at each of the layouts and discuss when each layout might be most beneficial to your needs.

The Recent Activity Dashboard layout

The **Recent Activity Dashboard** will show users everything that has happened within your course that they might have missed, for example, new assignments, discussions, or grades that have been posted. You might consider using this course home page layout with students who you know have taken online courses previously and are familiar with accessing course content online.

- The **Recent Activity Dashboard** is very similar to the update streams on social media sites such as **Twitter**, **Facebook**, **Tumblr**, or **Instagram**. The similarities to these sites can help more technologically savvy students feel at ease with accessing your course and keeping up with their responsibilities.

- If you have students in your class with less experience in online learning, you might want to consider one of the other course home page layouts that offer a more stable and sequential presentation of material.

For the **Recent Activity Dashboard,** you do not need to do anything once you select that option as your home page; it will automatically display recent events once the course begins. Your students will need to access the course content using the navigation links you have chosen for the left-side menu, and the course content will not be explicitly or consistently displayed when students open the home page to your course. Again, this layout would be well suited for technologically experienced students who are familiar with accessing content online.

The custom-designed content page layout

The next option, **Pages Front Page**, will allow you to create a content page that includes anything you would like to include. Most often, the content of a custom-designed welcome page contains welcome information, instructions, and links to course content. When you select this option from the drop-down menu and click on **Save**, you will see two buttons appear to the right of your course name on the home page, as shown in the following screenshot:

To edit your custom home page, complete the following steps:

1. Click on the **Edit** button.

2. From there, you will see a screen that includes the **Rich Content Editor** that we discussed in depth during *Chapter 2, Building Your Canvas Course*. You can add as much information as you would like, but it's generally best to keep the home page as simple, straightforward, and concise as possible. While you are editing, your Rich Content Editor might look something like what is shown in the following screenshot:

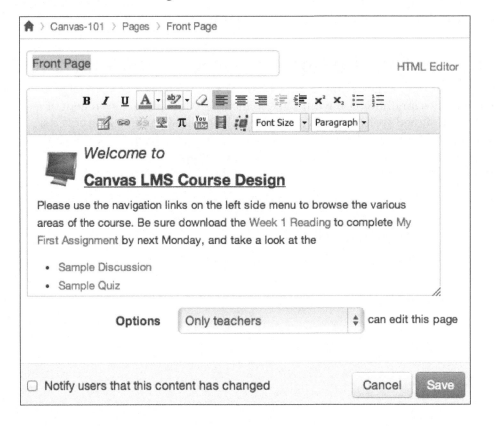

3. After you have finished editing your custom page, click on **Save** at the bottom of the screen.

4. After you have saved your page, it will appear as the home page for your course. You can always edit your page by clicking on the **Edit** button on the top of the home page.

You can also edit this page by clicking on the **Pages** tab in the left-side menu. You will see the front page of your course with an **Edit** button at the top. In addition, you will also see a button that will let you view all pages. If you click on this button, you will see a list of all of the content pages that have been created as well as a **+ Page** button in the top-right corner that will let you create new content pages. These options are shown in the following screenshot:

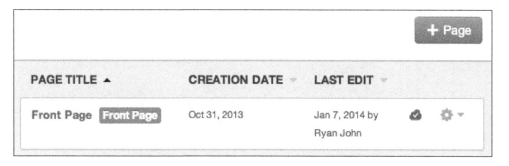

At this point, the only content page that has been created is the **Front Page**, which is the default name of your course home page. You might also wish to set up other content pages with further instructions and content. This type of course design allows you to basically create a completely customized course that students work through just like any other website on the Internet. Once you have created a page, it will show up when you click on the **Pages** navigation link on the left-side menu. From the **Pages** page, you will be able to view, edit, and delete any content pages you have created:

- Using a custom-designed content page as your course home page layout is great for teachers who are comfortable with using the Rich Content Editor.

- This allows students to experience a personalized, unique welcome to the course when they log in that can offer clear instructions for how to participate in the course.

- You can easily embed important content that students will need for success in the course directly on the home page with the Rich Text Editor, and you may choose to design your course using other content pages that will allow students to explore and experiment with the course content at their own pace.

While you certainly do not have to create multiple content pages, you might wish to use pages in conjunction with materials and assignments in the next type of home page layout that we will discuss, which is the **Course Modules** layout.

The Course Modules layout

The **Course Modules** layout allows you to sequence material very clearly on the home page so that students can begin participating immediately when they first log in:

1. If you select this option from the **Edit Homepage** drop-down menu and then click on **Save**, the options and instructions pictured in the following screenshot will appear on your home page.

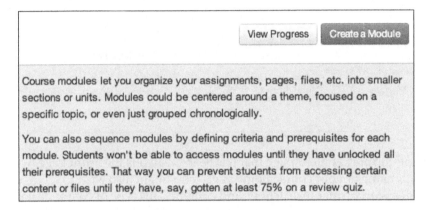

2. Click on the **Create a Module** button and a pop-up window will appear that allows you to name the module, choose to lock the module until a certain date, and choose to require students to move through the content within the module sequentially. The following screenshot shows you an example of what the first course module might look like:

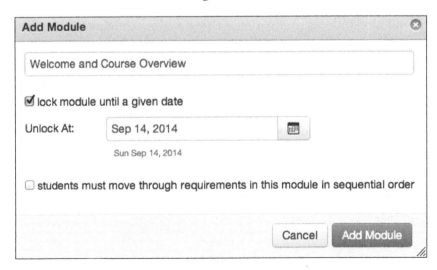

3. When you have adjusted the settings to your liking, click on **Add Module** to create your first module. The pop-up window will close and reveal your new home page with an empty first module.

4. To add content to the module, click on the plus icon to the right of the module title bar, as shown in the following screenshot:

5. The pop-up window that opens will allow you to select the content you have created from your course and insert it into the module. For example, to include a quiz you have created, select **Quiz** from the top drop-down menu, and then select the desired quiz from the list that appears below it.

6. To indent the item within the module for aesthetic clarity, you can select the level of indentation from the bottom drop-down menu. In the following screenshot, you can see that a **Quiz** is being added to the **Welcome and Course Overview** module. The specific quiz is the **Sample Quiz**, and the **Indentation** will be **Indent 1 Level**:

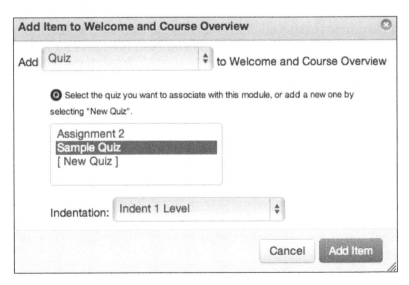

7. Once you click on the **Add Item** button, you will see the item appear in the module on the home page. You can add as many items as you would like to each module, and you can create new modules by clicking on the **Create Module** button at the top of the home page.

8. To rearrange items within a module, click-and-drag the dots that appear to the left of the item name as shown in the following screenshot:

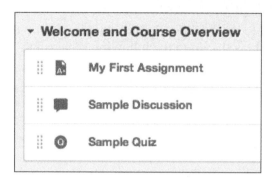

By creating course modules, you are able to organize content together sequentially, with the capability to set prerequisites that ensure that students move through the through the content in a particular order. As you add content to modules, the options to edit will expand and allow you to set requirements for each item within the module. To adjust the restrictions and prerequisites for each module, complete the following steps:

1. Click on the gear icon to the right of the module name and click on **Edit**.

2. Once you have added content to the module, you will see a new option to **Add Requirement** that students will need to complete in order to move past the module in the course. You can add requirements for as many items as you like, or you can allow students to move through the modules at their own pace. The following screenshot displays requirements for three assignments that have been added to a module:

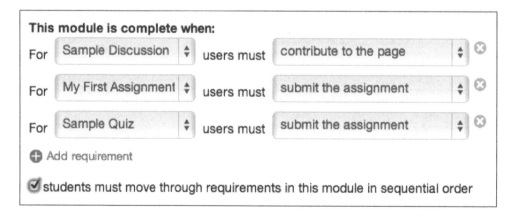

3. When you have adjusted the settings to your liking, click on **Update Module**.

The **Course Modules** home page layout offers a clear, concise sequence through which your students can move while allowing you to incorporate your own teaching style by adjusting the settings. You may wish to allow students to move through each module at their own pace or require them to move through the content sequentially.

When you organize content into modules and open the page for an item, **Next** or **Previous** arrows appear at the bottom of each item's page that allow students to move to the next item in the module sequentially. For example, if you have placed an assignment between two other items within a module, arrows will appear at the bottom of the assignment page that will allow you to navigate to the preceding and subsequent items in the module with one easy click, as shown in the following screenshot:

You may wish to only reveal content one week at a time or to make it all available from the first day, so students can move as quickly or slowly as they wish. You may also wish to add content pages that explain the instructions for the module to each module. The combinations and options are numerous, and you have the freedom to utilize as many or as few of the options made available to you depending on your needs and comfort level.

The Assignment List layout

The **Assignment List** layout allows your students to see a clear list of the assignments you have created for the course in a chronological order by the due date. When you select this course home page layout option and click on **Save**, you will see the list of assignments appear as the new home page for your course, as shown in the following screenshot:

Upcoming Assignments

Sample Discussion	Sep 19 at 11:59pm	out of 100
Sample Quiz	Sep 19 at 11:59pm	out of 100
My First Assignment	Sep 19 at 11:59pm	out of 100

The sample assignments in the preceding example were all set for the same due date at the same time, but your assignments would be displayed in a chronological order.

This course home page layout would be an excellent idea for a live course with online expectations; students are able to log in and see the exact assignments they would need to complete with the due date and point value clearly listed in one place. Content delivered during the live class would allow students to successfully complete the assignments by logging in to Canvas and then completing and submitting their work for you to grade. Of course, this layout would also be suited for the other types of classes you may be teaching, and you may choose to use this layout depending on your teaching style and the needs of your students.

The Syllabus layout

The **Syllabus** course home page layout is very similar to the **Assignment List** layout, but includes a custom syllabus description above the assignment list as well as course syllabus information added to the bottom of the right-side menu of the new home page. Once you select this option as your course home page and click on **Save**, you will see the course syllabus information appear in the right-side menu of the home page with an **Edit Syllabus Description** button above the course calendar. The syllabus description gives you the option to create a custom description for your course, which could act just as the welcome page you might design if you were to choose the **Pages Front Page** layout. To customize your syllabus description, complete the following steps:

1. Click on **Edit Syllabus Description** on the right-side menu above the calendar and grading specifications will as shown in the following screenshot:

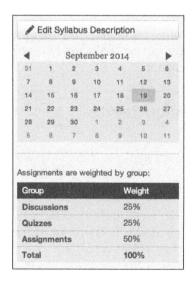

2. From there, a page will open with the Rich Content Editor and you will be able to add a welcome message, write a syllabus description, and embed any content you might wish to include.

3. Click on **Update Syllabus** to save your course description, and it will appear above the assignment list on your new course home page.

This course home page layout is very well suited to any kind of course you may be teaching. It requires minimal work on your part in entering the syllabus description, and the course layout comes across very clearly to students at all levels of technological experience.

Adding course calendar events

Once you have picked a course home page layout and finished organizing the content of your course accordingly, you may wish to add other events to your course calendar that do not already appear as assignments within your course. Examples of events you may wish to add to your course calendar might include the following:

- Live class meetings
- Synchronous online meetings
- Field trips
- Special events (for example, student birthdays, holidays, lectures, or performances)

To add events to your calendar, you can either click on the **Calendar** link on the top menu or navigate back to the course setup checklist and click on **Add Course Calendar Events**.

Once you see your course calendar, you will see a plus sign icon at the top-right corner of the calendar grid. To create a new event, use the following instructions:

1. Click on the plus sign icon at the top-right corner of the calendar page. A pop-up window will open that will allow you to create a new calendar event.

2. Notice that the tabs at the top of the pop-up window allow you to create an **Event** or create a new **Assignment**.

3. To add an event, stay on the **Event** tab and enter the **Title** of the event, the **Date** of the event, the times **From** which the event will run, and to which **Calendar** you would like to add the event. These options are shown in the following screenshot:

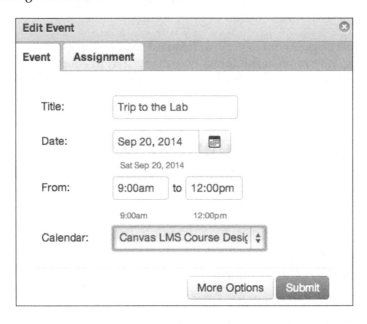

4. If you would like to add more information to the event, you can click on the **More Options** button to view a page with the Rich Content Editor that will allow you to embed content for the event you are creating.

5. Once you are finished entering the information for your new event, click on the **Submit** button. The pop-up window will close, and your new event will appear on the calendar you selected.

Notice on the right-side menu that you have the option to change the calendar you are viewing. Your name will appear with a colored check box, as will the names of the courses you are teaching, as shown in the following screenshot. You can check or uncheck each calendar to see what items appear for each calendar. Students enrolled in a course will be able to see the calendar for that course, whereas only you will be able to see your personal calendar.

Testing your course with Student View

Congratulations! You've made it through building your first Canvas course. Before we move on to publishing, it is always a good idea to start on the home page of your course and work your way through the entire course the same way a student would. Canvas has designed a **Student View** feature that allows you to see exactly what your course will look like to students. To access your course through **Student View**, complete the following steps:

1. Click on the **Settings** link on the left-side menu of your course.

2. On the settings page, click on the **Student View** button at the top of the right-side menu, as shown in the following screenshot:

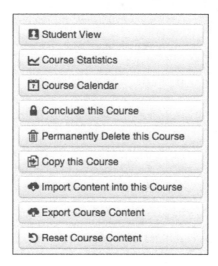

3. From there, you will see your course home page in **Student View**. Notice the message at the bottom of your screen that lets you know **You are currently logged into Student View**.

4. While you are in **Student View**, you can view all of the areas of your course that your students are able to see. You can even view and submit assignments as a test student, which will show up privately in your Gradebook as a *test student*. However, keep in mind that anything you post publicly within the course, such as a reply on a discussion post, will be visible to real students under the name **Test Student**.

5. When you have worked your way through your entire course, you are able to reset the test student feature by clicking on the **Reset Student** button at the bottom of the screen. This will delete any mock assignments you may have submitted while in **Student View**, and it will allow you to view the course afresh as if you were a new student.

6. Once you are finished checking your course in **Student View**, click on the **Leave Student View** button at the bottom of your screen. The following screenshot shows you the **Reset Student** button and the **Leave Student View** buttons that appear at the bottom of your screen while in student view:

Before you publish your course, it is a very good idea to go through your course one final time, either in student view or in regular view, to make sure your course is totally ready to go live:

- Double-check that everything is organized the way you want it to be, and that all of the content your students will need is embedded and ready to go
- Proofread all of your instructions and double-check all of your due dates

Once you are satisfied that everything in your course is set up accurately and correctly, you are ready to publish your course.

Publishing your course

To publish your course, complete the following steps:

1. Go to the course home page. At the top of the page, you will see the following message:

2. If you click on the **published** link, you will see the course setup checklist appear with the bottom **Publish Course** option selected. From the course setup checklist, go ahead and click on the **Publish Course** button in the course setup checklist, as shown in the following screenshot:

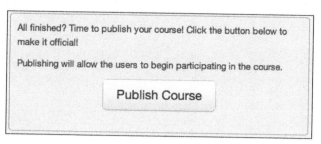

When you click on the **Publish Course** button, your course will be live. All of the students and observers who have not already received invitations to join the course will receive e-mails instructing them to join the course. You are now ready to begin teaching your course!

Summary

In this chapter, we completed the construction of your course. We started by adding participants to the course, and we discussed the various roles participants can fulfill within your course: **Students**, **Teachers**, **TAs**, **Designers**, and **Observers**. Next, we discussed how to manage participants in your course and began to reorganize the appearance of your course by selecting which **Navigation Links** your students will see on the left-side menu. We discussed the various types of home page layouts available to you based on your needs, including the **Recent Activity Dashboard**, the **Custom Content Page** layout, the **Course Modules**, the **Assignment List** layout, and the **Assignment List with Syllabus**. Finally, we explored the Canvas **Calendar**, reviewing your course in the **Student View** mode, and learned how to **Publish** your course.

In the next chapter, we will cover topics that include how to communicate with users in your course using Canvas, how to use the *Gradebook*, and how to create and facilitate synchronous video meetings with all users within your course.

4

Teaching Your Canvas Course

Now that you've made it through building your course, you can breathe a sigh of relief and feel confident that your planning and hard work will pay off. From this point on, we begin the actual teaching of your course, where your finely honed skills as an educator will guide you and your students through the course content to success. While the Canvas platform for teaching and learning may be new to you, it is important to keep in mind everything you know from being a real-life teacher. Keep the following basics in mind:

- Getting to know your students
- Maintaining open communication
- Providing insightful feedback
- Fielding questions and concerns

Everything you know from your experience as an educator can and should be transferred to your Canvas course, and this chapter will help you make that happen through the medium of Canvas. As a teacher, you know that maintaining open communication with your students is key. To begin, let's explore the **Conversations** messaging feature of Canvas.

Communicating through Conversations

To facilitate direct communication between users, as opposed to general information posted within a course, the Conversations feature in Canvas allows you to send messages directly to individual users or to groups of users. While we will discuss how to send messages to multiple users in this section, we will later discuss the **Announcements** feature, which is a more practical option when disseminating information to everyone within a specific course. Canvas organizes individual messages into conversations based upon the users involved in the exchange, so in the following sections, the term "message" refers to an individual entry of a conversation.

Most of the messages that appear in the Conversations feature of Canvas are messages that users send directly to one another. However, as you get further into your course, you will notice that other messages, such as comments left on submitted assignments, also appear in your conversations. The following sections will help familiarize you with the layout of the Conversations feature as well as how to compose, send, and organize conversations.

Learning the layout of Conversations

To access your conversations, click on the **Inbox** link in the top-right menu next to your name. Notice that when you have a new message waiting in your inbox, you will see a notification bubble next to the **Inbox** link, indicating how many new messages you have. The following screenshot displays the **Inbox** link as well as a new message notification:

When the Conversations page is opened, you will see two main parts to the screen. On the left-hand side, you will see the list of conversations with which you are involved. On the right-hand side of your screen, you will see the actual message body with the thread of messages contained within the selected conversation. As a brand new Canvas user, you will most likely not be involved with any conversations, so the list of conversations on the left-hand side of your screen will appear blank. Once you begin receiving messages, the list of conversations will grow to display each conversation with which you are involved. Note that you will not see the messages within a conversation until you select the conversation from the list of conversations on the left-hand side. The following screenshot shows you the top menu of the Conversations page as well as a list of conversations on the left-hand side and a **No Conversations Selected** message on the right-hand side where the message body would appear:

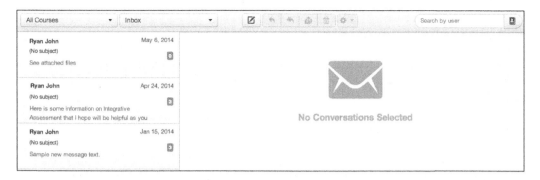

The first item on the left-hand side of the top menu on the Conversations page is a drop-down menu that allows you to view messages from **All Courses** or select a specific course from which you would like to view messages. This feature can help you stay organized if you are teaching multiple courses using Canvas, as you will be able to focus on viewing or responding to messages from users in one course at a time.

The next option to the right-hand side is a drop-down menu that allows you to select which kinds of conversations you are viewing. The following list describes what types of messages fall under each option of this drop-down menu:

- **Inbox**: Selecting this option will display all conversations in which you are involved.

- **Unread**: Selecting this option will display all conversations that contain new messages you have not yet read.

- **Starred**: Selecting this option will display all conversations that you have starred or marked as important. We will learn how to star conversations shortly.

- **Sent**: Selecting this option will display all of the messages you have sent to other users.

- **Archived**: Selecting this option will display all messages you have archived or stored away out of your inbox. We will learn how to archive and unarchive conversations shortly.

As you become more comfortable using the Conversations feature of Canvas, you will develop your own organizational style of maintaining your inbox in the same way you probably have with any e-mail accounts you use. These options will help you quickly and easily find what you are looking for as you begin sending and receiving messages with users in your courses.

To the right-hand side of the drop-down menus, you will see a number of icons that allow you to complete various tasks that involve your conversations. These icons offer many of the same functions as a standard e-mail client, including **Compose a new message**, **Reply**, **Reply all**, **Archive**, **Delete**, and **More Options**. Hover your mouse over each icon to see a textual description of the icon. These icons will be the central part of your message experience, as they allow you to complete all of the basic tasks required to send and receive messages using Canvas. If an icon appears as a gray outline, you will need to select a message before that option becomes available.

At the right-hand side of the top menu, you will see a search bar to **Search by user**. This feature can be very helpful for quickly finding a message from a specific user, especially if the message or conversation is not very recent. Now that we have familiarized ourselves with the layout of the Conversations page, let's move on to composing and sending messages to other Canvas users.

Composing and sending a message

To compose a message, perform the following steps:

1. On the top menu of the Conversations page, click on the **Compose a new message** icon, as pictured in the following screenshot:

2. In the pop-up window that appears, select the course in which the user(s) you would like to message are participating from the drop-down menu, as pictured in the following screenshot:

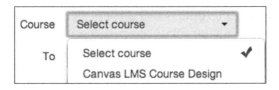

3. Next, type in the name or names of the users you wish to send a message to in the **To** field. If you click on the icon to the right-hand side of the **To** field, you can find and choose users from the many options that appear, as pictured in the following screenshot:

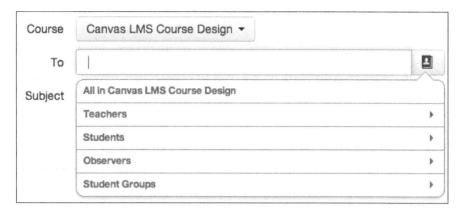

4. Once you have selected the desired user(s) to be included in the message, enter the topic of your message in the **Subject** field.

5. If you are sending a message to multiple users and would like to disable the **Reply all** feature, you can check the box next to **Send individual messages**. This essentially functions in the same way as the **blind carbon copy** (BCC) feature in standard e-mail clients.

6. Next, you can type the text of your message in the large text box below the **Course**, **To**, and **Subject** fields.

7. When the text of your message is complete, you can choose **Add an attachment** or **Record an audio or video comment** by clicking on the icons on the bottom-left corner of the pop-up window. The **Add an attachment** option will open the Documents folder of your computer, from which you can select the desired attachment. The **Record an audio or video comment** option below the text box will open the same dialog box as you saw in the Media option within the Rich Content Editor that we discussed in *Chapter 2, Building Your Canvas Course*. Using this feature, you can record a new audio or video comment or upload an existing audio or video file to send along with your message.

8. When you are satisfied with your message, click on the **Send** button in the bottom-right corner of the pop-up window to send it to the specified users.

Organizing conversations

When your course has started, you will begin receiving messages from users in your course through the Conversations feature of Canvas. In order to maintain open and prompt communication with participants of your course, you should make sure to keep your conversations organized. The first two drop-down menus on the top menu of the Conversations page will help you keep track of conversations that fall under various categories. The following section focuses on organizing conversations into the options of the second drop-down menu, which is pictured in the following screenshot:

Marking conversations as unread

As we discussed while learning the layout of the Conversations feature, the **Inbox** link in the top-right menu of Canvas will alert you to new messages by displaying a circle icon next to the **Inbox** link that shows you the number of new messages you have received. On the Conversations page, you will see a blue dot to the left-hand side of each conversation that contains a new message, such as the conversation in the following screenshot:

After you have selected and read a new message, this blue dot will disappear. If you would like to mark the conversation as unread again, perform the following steps:

1. Hover your mouse over the conversation you wish to mark as unread.

2. Click on the circular outline that appears, as pictured next to **(No subject)** in the following screenshot:

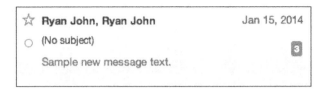

3. Once you click on the circular outline, the message will be marked as unread and will appear if you select **Unread** from the drop-down filter on the top menu.

4. You can also mark a conversation as unread by selecting the conversation, clicking on the **More options** icon from the top menu, and then selecting **Mark as unread** from the drop-down menu that appears.

Starring conversations

When you hover your mouse over a conversation, you will also see the outline of a star appear next to the users involved with the message. You can star a particularly important message or a message that requires further response or follow-up. This option serves the same purpose as flagging a message in many standard e-mail clients. To star a message, complete the following steps:

1. Hover your mouse over the conversation you wish to star.

2. Click on the outline of a star that appears next to the users involved with the message.

3. Once you click on the starred outline, a yellow star will appear and the conversation will be starred. The conversation will now appear if you select **Starred** from the drop-down filter on the top menu.

4. You can also star a conversation by selecting the conversation, clicking on the **More options** icon on the top menu, and then selecting **Star** from the drop-down menu that appears.

Viewing sent messages

Should you wish to view messages that you have sent, select **Sent** on the second dropdown of the top menu. This will show you all messages that you have sent within any conversations with which you are involved.

Archiving and unarchiving conversations

As you are viewing and responding to messages, you may wish to archive certain conversations. Archiving conversations removes them from your inbox and the list of conversations but does not delete them. To archive a conversation, perform the following steps:

1. Select the conversation you wish to archive from the list of conversations on the left-hand side of your screen.

2. Click on the **Archive** icon on the top menu, as pictured in the following screenshot:

3. The conversation will be removed from your **Inbox** and will appear if you select **Archived** from the drop-down filter on the top menu.

If you need to unarchive a conversation, perform the following steps:

1. Select **Archived** from the second dropdown on the top menu.

2. Find the conversation you wish to move back to your **Inbox** and select it from the list of conversations on the left-hand side.

3. Once the conversation is selected, click on the **Unarchive** icon, which is pictured in the following screenshot:

4. Once you click on the **Unarchive** icon, the conversation will be moved back to your inbox.

Deleting conversations

Once you have read and responded to messages within a conversation, you might wish to delete your copy of the conversation. Note that when you delete a conversation, you only delete the conversation from your account. The messages within the conversation will still be available to other users involved with a conversation. To delete a conversation, perform the following steps:

1. Select the conversation from the list of conversations on the left-hand side of your screen.

2. Click on the **Delete** icon that looks like a trashcan on the top menu of the Conversations page.

3. You might see a pop-up message that asks you whether you are sure you want to delete your copy of the conversation. The message indicates that this action cannot be undone. If you are sure that you would like to delete the conversation, click on **OK**. This message may look different depending on the web browser you are using.

4. After you have clicked on the **Delete** icon and confirmed your action, the message will no longer be available to you.

Now that we've looked at how to communicate directly with users in your course, let's move on to communicating publicly with everyone in your course using the Announcements feature.

Posting announcements

The Announcements feature of Canvas allows you to post information publicly in your course. Posting Announcements is a quick and easy way to communicate with all participants in your class. The information you post can then be easily referenced from the Announcements navigation link on the left-hand side menu of your course.

To make an announcement, complete the following steps:

1. Click on the **Announcements** tab on the left-hand side menu of your course.

2. In the top-right corner of the page that opens, you will see the **Make an announcement** option. Click on this option, and a page will open up with the Rich Content Editor.

3. In the **Topic Title** bar at the top of the new announcement, type in the title of the announcement you would like to make.

4. In the textbox of the Rich Content Editor, enter the information you would like to post publicly within your course.

5. You can add an attachment using the option below the textbox, and you can adjust the options as you see fit for the announcement.

6. When you are satisfied with your post, click on **Save** in the bottom-right corner.

When you have posted your announcement, it will appear on the **Announcements** page of your course. Announcements have the same features and functionalities as a discussion board post, so participants in the course will be able to reply to the post with comments (unless you decide to select the **Close for Comments** option). You can edit your announcement or adjust the options for your announcement using the icons in the top-right corner of the **Announcements** page.

To ensure that participants in your course have a positive and productive experience, it is best to utilize the communication features of Canvas consistently and predictably. You may choose to only use the Conversations or **Announcements** features of Canvas individually, or you may wish to convey certain types of information to participants through a combination of both features. Establishing open communication with your students at the beginning of your course is very important, as is maintaining open communication with participants when you begin grading their assignments using the **Gradebook** and the **SpeedGrader** features of Canvas.

Using the Gradebook

When students begin submitting assignments for your course, you will need to start viewing, assessing, and grading their assignments as well as offering them feedback on their work. Depending on the type of course you are teaching, submissions might be electronic or in hard copy, and your feedback to students might be electronic or in person.

Accessing the Gradebook and entering grades

The Gradebook in Canvas has all the basic functionality of a traditional analog gradebook, but it offers you a wide range of options that a traditional gradebook cannot. To access the Gradebook, you can click on the **Grades** link of the left-hand side menu within a course or on the **Grades** link on the top Canvas menu. Once the Gradebook has opened, you will see a grid with students' names along the left-hand side as well as their secondary ID, such as their e-mail address or student ID number. The following screenshot shows you a sample of a student name and secondary ID that appears on the left-hand side of the Gradebook grid:

Student Name	Secondary ID
Test Student	180c059d2d315a...

In the center of the Gradebook grid, you will see assignment names listed across the top with students' grades for each assignment listed underneath next to their names. If students have made submissions for particular assignments, you will see an icon indicating their submission within the Gradebook grid. Different icons appear for different assignment submission types—you can hover your mouse over any unfamiliar icons for a text description of the icon's function. For assignments that have not yet been submitted, you will see a dash. In the following screenshot, the icons under **Sample Discussion** and **My First Assignment** indicate an ungraded submission, the **95** under **Sample Quiz** indicates the graded score, and the dash under **My Second Assignment** indicates that the student has not yet made a submission:

| Sample Discussion | Sample Quiz | My First Assignment | My Second Assignment |
Out of 100	Out of 100	Out of 100	Out of 100
💬	95	T	-

To manually enter or change a grade within the Gradebook grid, click on the grade or dash under the assignment you wish to adjust. The grade or dash will turn into a textbox in which you will be able to manually type in the grade and then press *Enter* or return on your keyboard to save it. For example, if you were to click on the dash under **My Second Assignment** in the preceding screenshot, you would be able to enter a point value and then save it by pressing *Enter*. You will also notice that you have the option to use the up and down arrows that appear next to the textbox to adjust points for the grade instead of typing the grade in manually. Each type of assignment has a variety of grading options. For example, certain quiz types such as multiple choice, true/false, or fill in the blank are automatically graded when students complete them. Quizzes with essay or short answer responses will require manual grading through the SpeedGrader, which we will discuss shortly.

Along the right-hand side of the Gradebook, you will see the total averages for each assignment group as well as the students' overall average for all of their completed assignments. The following screenshot indicates the percent average for each assignment group as well as the student's total average for all completed assignments:

Discussions	Quizzes	Assignments	Total
86%	95%	81%	87.3%

Once you begin using the Gradebook, you might wish to use the options located above the Gradebook grid. If you click on the gear icon that appears above the column of students' names, a drop-down menu will open with a number of options, as pictured in the following screenshot:

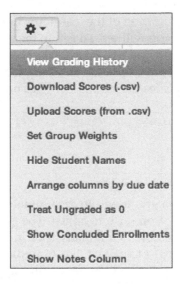

These options allow you to customize the way your Gradebook appears as well as other helpful features such as downloading scores or viewing the history of your grading. You may experiment with these options and set your Gradebook preferences to your liking.

 Another useful viewing feature of the Gradebook is the filter bar located above the assignment groups in the top-right corner of the Gradebook. You can filter the Gradebook grid to only display students that match the criteria you type into this bar.

Now that you are more familiar with the layout of the Gradebook and how to manually enter grades into the Gradebook grid, let's move on to accessing students' online submissions through the SpeedGrader. For assignments that require online submissions, such as **Sample Discussion** and **My First Assignment** in the previous screenshots, you will need to open the **SpeedGrader** to view the submission and utilize the grading options for various assignments.

Accessing and using a SpeedGrader

The **SpeedGrader** in Canvas allows you to quickly view students' submissions, assess their work, enter a grade, and offer feedback for individual assignments. To view a student's submission in the SpeedGrader from the Gradebook, perform the following steps:

1. Click on the small blue icon that appears in the corner of the grid when you hover your mouse over the student's submission. This icon appears on the right-hand side of the dark thought bubble in the center of the following screenshot:

2. From here, a dialog box will appear over the Gradebook that shows you the student's submission, as pictured in the following screenshot:

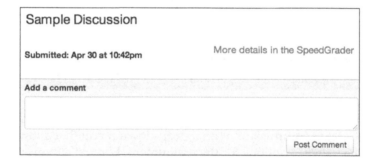

3. Click on the **More Details in the SpeedGrader** link that appears in this dialog box to view the entire assignment in the SpeedGrader.

You can also access the SpeedGrader from the **To Do** list that appears on your Canvas home page and on the home pages for each course you teach. The **To Do** list appears on the right-hand side of the course home page with the calendar and **Coming Up** sections. As students submit assignments, you will see the name of each assignment appear under your **To Do** list along with the number of assignments that need to be graded. To open the SpeedGrader for assignments that need to be graded, you can click on the assignment link that appears on your **To Do** list.

Once you have opened the SpeedGrader, you will see four main sections of the screen that allow you to complete various tasks for grading an assignment. Perform the following steps to utilize each section of the screen in grading your assignments:

1. In the top-left corner, you will see the student's name displayed with arrows on either side, as shown in the following screenshot. If you click on these arrows, you can navigate through all of the students' submissions for the selected assignment:

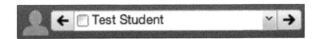

2. Across the top pane of the **SpeedGrader** page, you will find links for **Gradebook**, **Course Home**, assignment page, **Mute Assignment**, **Settings**, and **Help** along with specifics for the selected assignment and how many submissions you have graded. If you click on **Mute Assignment**, a pop-up window will appear, explaining that muting an assignment will stop notifications about the assignment and limit accessibility of the muted assignment. From there, you can choose to mute the assignment or leave it unmuted for students to access. You can adjust the sorting and viewing options by clicking on the **Settings** link, and you can find help with the SpeedGrader by clicking on the **Help** link. The following screenshot shows you the top menu of the SpeedGrader:

3. In the bottom-left corner of the **SpeedGrader** page, you will see a display of the student's **Submission** with a drop-down menu that allows you to adjust the viewing options for the assignment. For text submissions, **Paper View** allows you to see the student's text submission with formatting and embedded content, while **Plain Text View** removes any formatting and embedded content to display plain text. The following screenshot displays a sample text submission in **Paper View**:

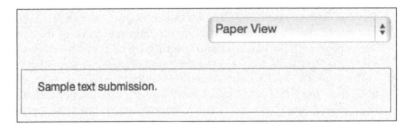

4. On the right-hand side of the **SpeedGrader** page, you will see the **Assessment** and feedback section, where you can view the submission date/time, give a grade, view and utilize a rubric to assign a grade, and leave feedback for the individual student. Notice that you have the option to **Add a Comment**, **Attach** a file, record a media comment (audio or video), or use speech recognition to dictate a written comment. To utilize a rubric within the SpeedGrader, you will have to create a rubric for the assignment, which we will discuss in *Chapter 5, Exploring Special Features*. The following screenshot displays the assessment and feedback options that appear on the right-hand side of the SpeedGrader:

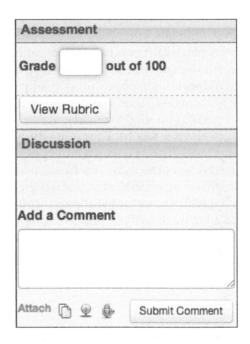

5. When you have finished reviewing the submission, assigning a grade, and providing feedback, you can click on **Submit Comment** to save any written feedback and then click on the arrows to the right- or left-hand side of the student's name in the top-left corner to move to the next submission. The SpeedGrader autosaves your grades, so if you do not need to leave a written comment, you can enter the grade and then navigate to the next student's assignment, and your work will automatically be saved.

6. When you have finished grading all submissions for a particular assignment, you can use the links at the top of the page to navigate back to the Gradebook or the course home page.

If you would like to download all of the submissions that students have made for a particular assignment, you can navigate to the assignment page and click on the **Download Submissions** link that appears on the right-hand side menu of the assignment page. All of the submission files will be downloaded to your computer in a ZIP file; at which point, you can open each submission to make comments or corrections. You can then return to the assignment page and click on the **Re-Upload Submissions** link that also appears on the right-hand side menu. Once you have re-uploaded the altered submissions, students will receive a copy of their submission with your comments or corrections.

As you work through your students' assignment submissions, keep in mind the kind of feedback that you traditionally offer. Most likely, you are used to giving written feedback on assignments, which you have the capability of doing directly within Canvas. Since Canvas offers you the ability to record audio or video feedback, consider taking advantage of this unique opportunity to appeal to the non-visual learners you may have in your classes. After you have viewed an assignment submission and assigned a grade, you might consider starting an audio or video recording as you verbally speak your feedback for your students, and then attach that recording to their assignment. This is a wonderful opportunity to reach out to students who do their best when processing information aurally or by making personal connections through seeing a video of you speaking directly to them. Canvas allows you to reach a wider variety of students through the features it offers, so make sure that you take advantage of these opportunities as they arise during your course. In addition to offering assignment feedback, you can consider setting up synchronous online meetings with your class through the **Conferences** feature.

Setting up synchronous meetings using Conferences

If you are teaching a fully online course, synchronous online meetings during which all members of your class are present online can be a huge benefit to the teaching and learning that takes place within your course. A synchronous online meeting allows all students and teachers involved in your course to participate in a virtual classroom, much like a conference call. Each member of the class logs in to the conference and connects to everyone else in the class; you are free to lead a presentation or lecture during this time, or open the conference up for group discussions and questions. In addition to the audio communication possible through these meetings, you and your students can enable your webcams. So, everyone in the class can see and talk to each other at the same time, just as you would in a live classroom. You can even record meetings so students who are not able to be present are still able to see what happened during the meeting. Students are also able to set up their own conferences, so means of collaboration and cooperation are built into your students' Canvas experience. Synchronous meetings afford students the opportunity for direct contact with you and their classmates in a real-time setting. As online learning gains popularity, one of the biggest critiques from educators and students alike is the lack of personal contact present in most online courses—the **Conferences** feature allows you to personalize learning and build community among you and your students.

Creating a conference

To set up a conference, complete the following steps:

1. Click on the **Conferences** link on the left-hand side menu of your course.
2. On the **Conferences** page, you will see a blue button in the top-right corner of the page that reads **New Conference**. Click on this button to open a pop-up window that will allow you to set up a new conference.

3. The pop-up window that appears will allow you to configure the following elements of your conference:

    ○ **Name**: This will allow you to configure the name of your conference.

    ○ **Type**: This will allow you to configure the type of conference you would like to create. It refers to the external conferencing service you would like to use for your conference. Canvas has partnered with BigBlueButton as a conferencing service, so BigBlueButton will appear as the default conferencing service for you to use. You might see other conferencing options available, depending on the services your institution has integrated into Canvas.

    ○ **Duration**: This will allow you to configure the duration of your conference.

    ○ **Record**: This will allow you to configure the options to record your conference and to allow **No Time Limit** for long-running conferences.

    ○ **Description**: This will allow you to configure the description of your conference. This is the best place to include information about the **Date**, **Time**, and **Duration** of your conference to ensure that all participants in your course are present for the conference. You might wish to post an announcement or send out a message to all of the participants in your course.

    ○ **Invite All Course Members**: This will allow you to invite all course members to the conference.

4. Once you have adjusted all of the conference specifications to your liking, you can click on the **Create Conference** button in the bottom-right corner of the pop-up window. After you have created the conference, invited participants will receive a notification about the conference (depending on their notification settings), and the conference will be listed under the **New Conferences** section of the **Conferences** page.

Starting and facilitating your conference

To start your conference, complete the following steps:

1. Click on the **Start** button that appears on the right-hand side of the conference name under **New Conferences**, as shown in the following screenshot:

2. When you click on the **Start** button, a new tab or window will open in your web browser, and you will be taken to the BigBlueButton conferencing service website (or to the conferencing service you or your institution have configured to work within Canvas). Note that students will not be able to join the conference until after you click on **Start**. While the following section will show you how to facilitate a conference using BigBlueButton as an example, the functions covered appear in most standard conferencing services and will help you better understand the possibilities of synchronous meetings.

3. The new tab or window that opens in your web browser will log you in to the conference. You will see a dialog box appear, as pictured in the following screenshot, that asks for permission to access your built-in microphone and webcam or the external microphone and webcam you have connected to your computer. In order to participate and facilitate the conference, you will need to click on **Allow** so the service can access your microphone and webcam, as shown in the following screenshot:

4. Once you have clicked on **Allow** to enable the use of your microphone and webcam, you will see an **Audio Settings** dialog box. From this box, you can test and adjust the microphone you wish to use as well as test the speakers or headset you will be using. You must check the settings displayed in this box and then click on **Join Audio** in order to be heard during the conference. The **Audio Settings** dialog box is pictured in the following screenshot:

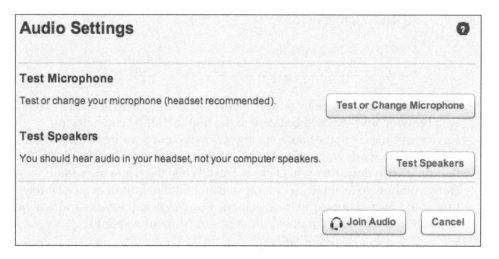

5. When you have joined the conference with your audio settings configured correctly, you will either hear other participants who are already in the conference or you will hear a message informing you that you are the only person in the conference so far.

Notice that when you hover your mouse over any item within the BigBlueButton page, an information box will pop up next to your cursor telling you what the item is. Use this to your advantage as you explore the conferencing screen to see what your options are.

The layout of the conferencing screen is broken down into a number of separate sections. First, the menu along the top of the screen allows you to control how you are participating in the conference and your language settings. You will also see the option to log out on the far right-hand side of this menu. The following screenshot displays the top menu of BigBlueButton:

To adjust your audio and video settings or share your desktop (that is, broadcast what you see on your computer screen to other participants' screens), click on the corresponding icons in the top-left corner. Make sure that your microphone and webcam are enabled when you begin a conference so all participants will be able to hear and see you. You can be sure that your microphone and webcam are working properly when you see a green check appear within the icons in the top-left menu, as displayed in the preceding screenshot. If you do not see this checkmark or if you need to adjust your microphone or webcam settings, you can click directly on the icons in the top-left menu which will open the settings for each option.

Next, look at the **Users** list on the left-hand side, which lists all of the participants involved in the conference by name. You can also see each user's status, specifically whether they are the presenter or a participant. As the facilitator of the conference, you are able to mute or unmute participants' microphones, which you will find is a useful tool to cut down on extraneous noise and feedback from certain users. Participants have the option to virtually raise their hand, at which time a small hand icon will appear next to their name so the presenter (presumably you to begin with) will see that that user would like to speak. Also, notice the **Settings** icon in the bottom-left corner of this section that gives you a variety of useful options when facilitating a conference, as pictured in the following screenshot:

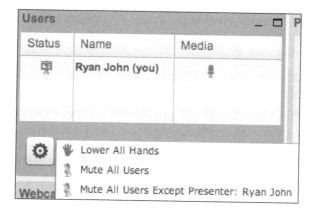

Below the **Users** list, you will see a **Webcams** preview window, which allows you to see the video you are broadcasting to other users, as pictured in the following screenshot, as well as previews of other users' webcam feeds. If you hover over a webcam preview, an icon will appear that allows you to mute or unmute that user:

In the center of your screen, you will see the **Presentation** area. The most useful place to begin when looking at this area as the presenter is the bottom-left corner, where you will see an **Upload Presentation** icon. To upload a presentation, perform the following steps:

1. Click on the **Upload Presentation** icon, and from there, a dialog box will open and you will be able to upload any previously constructed presentations that you might have created using programs such as PowerPoint or Keynote.

2. Click on **Select File** in the dialog box, locate the desired file on your computer, and then click on **Upload**.

3. From here, the presentation will appear within the center **Presentation** area, and you will be able to scroll through the slides using the arrows at the bottom. You will also be able to use the annotation tools along the right-hand side of the presentation area to mark up the presentation in real time.

When making a presentation during a class, you can speak through the presentation just as you would in a live class, and you can use the annotation tools to highlight or draw attention to specific aspects of the slide. The following screenshot offers an example of a slide with shapes and marks created using the annotation tools shown in the menu on the right-hand side of the presentation area:

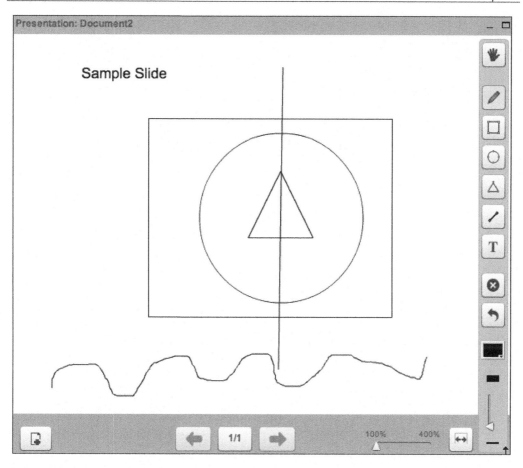

On the right-hand side of the Conference screen, you will see the **Chat** window, where you can post chat messages to the entire group or to specific users. Notice the **Public** and **Options** tabs at the top of this window. To post chat messages, complete the following steps:

1. To post a public chat message, type the message under the **Public** tab and click on **Send**.

2. To send a private chat message to an individual participant, select the participant from the **Options** tab and begin a private chat. The private chat will appear as a new tab where you can type your message and then click on **Send**. The following screenshot displays the **Chat** window, including the **Public** and **Options** tabs:

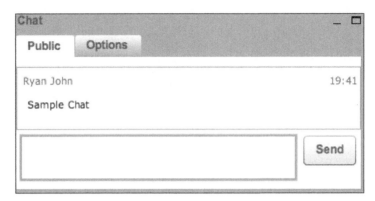

Finally, you will see a drop-down menu in the bottom-right corner of the screen that tells you that you are viewing the **Default** display view. The various display views change the layout of the conference depending on your needs, so you may choose to use a display view other then the default view, depending on how you intend to spend your time in the conference, as described in the following list:

- **Default**: This is a flexible view that allows you to see and manage all of the windows within the conference easily. This is useful when you are the sole presenter and facilitator of a conference.

- **Video Chat**: This view would be an excellent choice for a discussion-based class, wherein students had to keep the conference going by participating in the discussion. In most conferencing services, the person who is speaking will automatically appear on each user's screen when they speak as long as they are not muted. The chat, presentation, and user windows are not displayed in this view.

- **Meeting**: This view is helpful for situations when seeing people's faces and hearing their audio is important, but being able to see a presentation is also important. The webcam window takes up most of the screen, and the presentation and chat windows are visible.

- **Webinar**: This view works well for online class lectures wherein the presentation takes prominence, but seeing other participants and hearing their input is important. The presentation window takes up most of the screen, and the chat and webcam windows are visible.

- **Lecture Assistant**: This view can be used by a teacher's assistant to facilitate the class easily while you are presenting. The chat window takes up most of the screen in this view so the assistant can, for example, aid in solving technical difficulties with individuals during the lecture. All other windows are also visible in this view so the assistant can manage all aspects of the conference.

- **Lecture**: This view would be helpful when making a presentation with the help of an assistant to facilitate the conference. In the lecture view, the presentation area takes up the full screen and you are not able to see any of the other windows, so your focus can remain solely on the presentation.

When you have completed your conference, you can log out of the conference by clicking on the **Log Out** icon in the top-right corner. When you return to Canvas and view the **Conferences** page, the conference will appear under **Completed Conferences**.

Summary

In this chapter, we began by exploring the **Conversations** message feature of Canvas. We covered how to access messages by clicking on the **Inbox** link in the top-right menu. We were able to compose and send a message to various users and talked about the various ways to manage conversations, including how to mark as unread, star, archive, and delete conversations. Next, we discussed how to post announcements to your course. We then moved on to viewing assignments and grading using the **Gradebook** and the **SpeedGrader**. We began by accessing the **Gradebook** and the **SpeedGrader** and looked at how to view a submission for a specific student, how to assign them a grade, and how to offer feedback. Finally, we discussed setting up synchronous online meetings using the **Conferences** feature of Canvas by creating a sample BigBlueButton conference. We covered how to join the conference using your audio and then explored the various windows within the conferencing service, including **Top Menu**, the **Users** window, the **Webcam** preview section, **Presentation Area**, the **Chat** window, and the various **Display View** options.

At this point in your journey, we have successfully covered the basics of building and teaching your Canvas course. The next chapter will cover some of the extras and special features available to you through Canvas to further enhance your teaching. These options will allow you to bolster your students' understanding and achievement through learning to use the Canvas mobile device app, designating learning outcomes, developing assessment tools, integrating outside applications, and tracking activity within your course.

5
Exploring Special Features

Now that we have covered the basic skills required to create, build, design, and teach your Canvas course, let's look into some of the more advanced special features that Canvas has to offer. We'll begin by taking a look at the mobile application of Canvas that is available for your mobile devices. Next, we will figure out how to create collaborations between students that will allow them to work on documents together online. After this, we will learn how to set up learning outcomes and how to create rubrics within Canvas. Finally, we will take a look into how to use the powerful assessment and statistics tools within Canvas to monitor your students' progress, gauge and bolster student engagement, and map interactions between users from course to course.

Let's get started by learning how to access Canvas from your mobile device using the Canvas mobile app.

Using Canvas on your mobile devices

As mobile devices become more and more a part of modern-day life, Canvas has ensured that accessing your course and interacting with other participants is as easy as possible wherever you are with the mobile app version of Canvas. After you have finished building your course on a computer, the Canvas mobile app is a great way to keep up with your course from your smartphone, tablet, or other mobile device. Let's start by downloading the app, logging in, and then familiarizing yourself with the layout of the Canvas mobile app.

 Please note that the following screenshots are captured from an iPhone 5 that has iOS 7.1.1. The app is the Canvas by Instructure app, Version 3.2. The exact procedures and layout of the app may be different if you are using a different device, operating system, or app version.

Downloading and configuring the mobile app

To download the mobile app to your device, complete the following steps:

1. Open the app store on your device. Search for `canvas by instructure` within the search field in the app store.

2. If multiple apps appear in your search results, make sure to select the **Canvas by Instructure – the cloud native learning platform & learning management system** app so that you download the most current version of the app.

3. Once you have found the app, follow the standard procedure to download apps from the app store on your device. For the Apple Store, tap on **Free**, which will turn into an **Install** option. Tap on **Install** and you will be asked to enter your Apple ID credentials. Once you enter your Apple ID credentials, the app will begin downloading to your device. The following screenshot displays the app as it appears in the Apple Store, including the FREE option that you need to tap to begin the download:

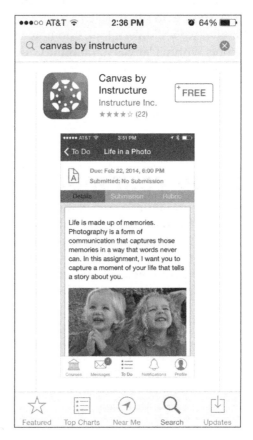

4. When the app download is complete, locate the app on your phone and tap on the icon to open it. The app icon is pictured in the following screenshot:

5. On the screen that opens, you will be asked to enter your Canvas URL. This is the same URL you would enter to access your Canvas account on a computer; so, it would either be your institution's Canvas site (usually similar to `https://institution.instructure.com`) or the Free for Teachers site (`https://canvas.instructure.com`). Tap the textbox that says **Enter your canvas URL**, type in your Canvas URL using the keyboard that appears, and then tap **Go** on your mobile keyboard or **Connect to Canvas Network**. The following screenshot shows the screen that will appear when you first open the Canvas mobile app:

6. Next, you will need to enter the e-mail address and password that you usually use to log in to Canvas on a computer. When you have entered your login credentials, tap **Login**. If you don't know your password, tap **I don't know my password**, then enter your e-mail address and tap **Request Password** to reset your password. The login screen is shown in the following screenshot:

7. Canvas will next ask permission to access your Canvas account through the mobile app. It will display the name and e-mail address associated with your account. To grant permission for the Canvas app to access your account and to do so in the future, tap the checkbox next to **Remember my authorization for this service** at the bottom of the screen and then tap **Login** as shown in the following screenshot:

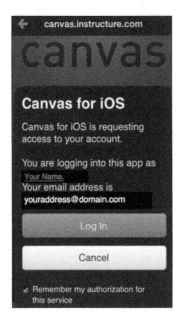

8. From here, the **Courses** screen will open within the app and you can begin to use the app.

Now that we have covered how to download and configure the Canvas app on your mobile device, let's move along to actually using the app to interact with content and users within your Canvas course.

Using the features of the mobile app

When your app first opens, you will see the **Courses** screen, which displays a list of the courses with which you are involved as pictured in the following screenshot:

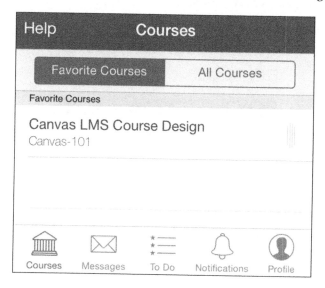

On the **Courses** screen that appears when you log in, notice the tab options to view **Favorite Courses** or **All Courses** — right now, you most likely only have one course listed, but when you have many courses within Canvas, you can find your courses using these tabs.

Looking at the bottom menu, you will see icons that allow you to quickly and easily view overviews of your **Courses, Messages, To Do** items, **Notifications**, and **Profile** options within the app. Let's now work our way through navigating and using the five main sections of the app that are shown along the bottom menu.

Navigating your course within the mobile app

The Canvas mobile app allows you to see and do most of the same things you are able to do within your course using a computer. To view and interact with the various sections and content of your course, complete the following steps:

1. Tap on your course to select it from the list of courses on the **Courses** screen that appears when you first open the mobile app.

2. When the course screen opens, you will see the **Home** page of your course. The home page layout you see within the mobile app will reflect the home page layout that you selected when you created your course. The following screenshot displays a **Syllabus** home page layout:

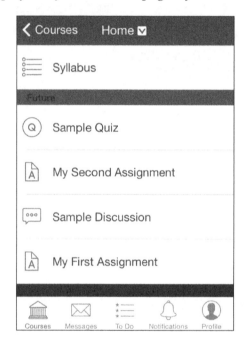

3. To view the full list of content in the course that is displayed on the left-hand side menu of your course when viewing it on a computer, tap **Home** at the top of the screen. The home screen will disappear and you will see the list of navigation links you designated for your course as pictured in the following screenshot:

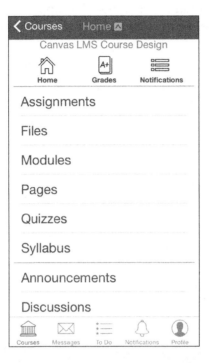

4. You can scroll through these options and explore the mobile version of each of these tabs. In addition, you can view the **Home** page and course **Notifications** by tapping the icons at the top of the screen. At the time of writing this, the **Grades** feature is not yet supported for instructors; however, your students will be able to view their grades in the course from within the mobile app by clicking on the **Grades** icon.

While the **Grades** feature of Canvas is not currently supported for instructors within the mobile app discussed here, you can download the SpeedGrader app for the iPad from the Apple Store. You can find instructions on how to use the SpeedGrader iPad app within Canvas Guides; we will discuss how to access and use this in *Chapter 6, Where to Go for Help*.

As we discussed in the previous chapters, taking time to explore the various features of Canvas allows you to gain personal insight into the inner workings of each feature through trial and error. Do not hesitate to use the same approach to learning the Canvas mobile app—take some time to explore and experiment with each feature. You might find that some of the features that appear on your course navigation list are not currently supported within the mobile app. As Instructure continues to develop, expand, and improve the Canvas mobile app, these features will most likely become available to you.

Let's now move on to discuss the next option along the bottom menu of the mobile app, the **Messages** feature, which allows you to utilize the conversations feature of Canvas.

Viewing and sending messages within the mobile app

Within the Canvas mobile app, it is easy to communicate with other Canvas users through the **Messages** feature, which functions in the same way as the **Conversations** feature of the web version of Canvas. To access and use the **Messages** feature of the mobile app, complete the following steps:

1. Tap on **Messages** on the bottom menu of the app. Your conversations inbox will open, and you will see options to view messages in your **Inbox**, your **Unread** messages, and your **Archived** messages, as pictured in the following screenshot:

2. Within your inbox, you will see the list of messages in your account with the most recent messages listed at the top of the screen. To open a message, tap on the message preview that includes the name of the sender and the beginning of the message.

3. Once you have read the selected message, you can tap the textbox that appears at the top of the message screen and type a response, as pictured in the following screenshot:

4. If you would like to add an attachment to your message, tap on the icon that looks like a paperclip. You have the option to **Choose from Library...**, **Take Photo or Video...**, or **Record Audio...** in order to attach a file. Choose the appropriate option and either locate the file on your device or follow the onscreen instructions to attach a new photo, video, or audio recording. The following screenshot displays the options that appear when you tap the attachment icon:

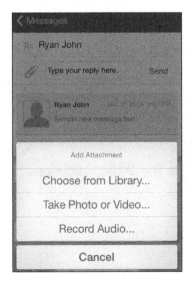

5. When you are satisfied with your response, tap **Send** and your reply will be sent.

Within the messaging feature of the mobile app, you can also compose new messages to other Canvas users. To compose a new message, complete the following steps:

1. Click on the compose icon in the top-right corner of the messaging screen, as outlined in the following screenshot:

2. The first step in composing a new message is adding recipients. Tap on the plus sign icon to the right of the **To:** field as pictured in the following screenshot:

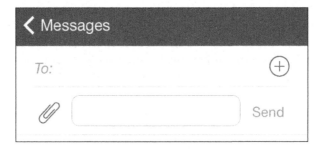

3. Next, tap on the **Search for recipients** bar that appears and type the name or names of those you wish to send a message. Suggestions will appear below the search bar—you can tap on the name of the desired recipient to add them to the message. When you have finished adding recipients, tap **Done** in the top-right corner, as shown in the following screenshot:

4. Next, you can type your message in the textbox that appears under the recipient list in the same way we replied to a message.

5. You can add an attachment in the same way to reply to a message.

6. When you are completely finished composing your message and attaching any items, tap the **Send** option to the right of the textbox to send your message.

Next, let's explore the **To Do** feature of the mobile app.

Using the To Do feature of the mobile app

The mobile app is helpful to easily view what you need to do for your course while you are away from your computer. To utilize the **To Do** feature of the mobile app, complete the following steps:

1. Tap on the **To Do** option on the bottom menu of the mobile app. You will see a list appear that identifies each task you need to complete for your course, as pictured in the following screenshot:

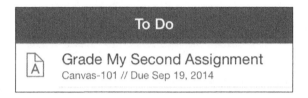

2. You can tap on each item in the **To Do** list to view the specifics of each task, such as the due date or the number of submissions received for an assignment. The following screenshot displays the options that appear when you tap on a **To Do** item:

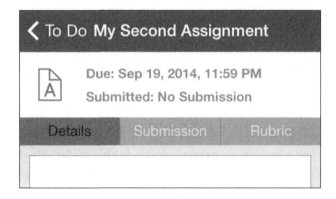

Most **To Do** items for instructors involve grading, which is currently not a supported feature in the mobile app. However, the **To Do** feature does offer you access to remind yourself of what you need to complete when you are back at your computer or able to use the SpeedGrader app for iPad mentioned previously.

Continuing on, we will take a look at the **Notifications** feature of the mobile app.

Accessing your notifications within the mobile app

While you are on the go, you can use the mobile app to view notifications of recent activity within your Canvas course. These notifications are based on the notification settings you configured when you set up your profile in *Chapter 1, Getting Started with Canvas*. To access your **Notifications**, complete the following steps:

1. Tap the **Notifications** option on the bottom menu of the mobile app. The screen that appears will display a list of recent activity within your course such as newly posted announcements or newly created assignments, as displayed in the following screenshot:

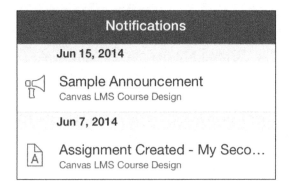

2. You can tap on any of the notifications that appear on the **Notifications** screen to view the full item, such as a new announcement or new assignment.

Now to review the final option of the bottom menu of the mobile app, viewing your **Profile**.

Viewing your profile within the mobile app

You are able to view the specifics of your Canvas profile within the mobile app. To see your Canvas profile from your mobile device, complete the following steps:

1. Tap on the **Profile** option on the bottom menu of the mobile app.

2. From here, you will see your profile picture, name, and e-mail address above a number of options. You can utilize the following options from the **Profile** feature of the mobile app:

   ° Tap on your profile picture to take a new profile picture using your device or to choose a new picture from the photo library on your device.

   ° Tap on **My Files** to see files that are associated with your Canvas profile.

   ° Tap on **About** to view the specifics of your account, including legal information from Canvas.

   ° Tap on **Help** to find help using the mobile app, which we will discuss in more depth in the next section.

   ° Tap **Logout** to remove your account information from the mobile app. If you choose this option, you will have to log in again next time you open the mobile app. The following screenshot displays the **Profile** feature of the mobile app and all of the functions described in the preceding bullets:

The final feature we will discuss for the Canvas mobile app is the **Help** feature.

Finding help within the Canvas mobile app

There are two ways you can access the **Help** feature within the Canvas mobile app:

- On the **Courses** screen, tap on **Help** in the top-left corner of the screen
- On the **Profile** screen, tap on the **Help** option

When you tap on the **Help** option, a screen will appear with a number of options from which you can choose. This screen is pictured in the following screenshot:

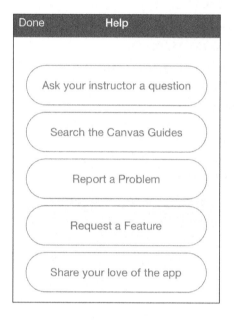

The following points describe the support available to you when you tap each option:

- **Ask your instructor a question**: This option is mainly for students who are having trouble or need to contact their instructor (you). This option opens a new message where students can type and send their problem to you as a message within Canvas.

- **Search the Canvas Guides**: This option allows you to browse and search some of the Frequently Asked Questions (FAQs) about the mobile app within the Canvas Guides. We will discuss the Canvas Guides in much more depth in *Chapter 6, Where to Go for Help*.

- **Report a Problem**: This option will open a new e-mail addressed to mobilesupport@instructure.com and will allow you to tell Canvas about any problems you might be encountering with the mobile app. This option works with the e-mail client app that you use on your device to send an e-mail to Canvas directly from your e-mail account.

- **Request a Feature**: This option will open a new e-mail addressed to mobilesupport@instructure.com and will allow you to send Canvas any ideas you might have for features that would improve the mobile app. This option works with the e-mail client app that you use on your device to send an e-mail to Canvas directly from your e-mail account.

- **Show your love of the app**: This option will open the app store for your device so that you can submit a review of the app to the app store.

Now that we have covered how to configure and navigate the Canvas mobile app, let's move back to your computer to discuss some of the more advanced special features of Canvas that allow you to customize and enhance the teaching and learning process. We'll start by taking a look at how to set up **Collaborations** between participants in your course.

Creating Collaborations

The **Collaborations** feature of Canvas allows you to set up ways in which your students can work together to create documents online. Through two integrated outside web tools, **Collaborations** allow you to set up documents that multiple users can access and edit together in real time from different locations. Some examples of situations in which you might choose to utilize the **Collaborations** feature of Canvas might be for planning group projects, full class note-taking, brainstorming ideas, signing up for activities, or writing a group paper to save and submit to a group assignment. In addition to teacher-created collaborations, students can use the **Collaborations** feature to create their own group documents as well by following the same steps described in this section.

Canvas allows you to set up group documents with **EtherPad** or with **Google Docs**. As mentioned on the **Collaborations** page within Canvas, EtherPad is better suited for use in situations where students need to contribute to the group document anonymously or without creating an individual outside account. For the purposes of this discussion, let's walk our way through setting up a collaboration using EtherPad as an example of how you might give your students the opportunity to work together using their existing Canvas accounts.

Google Docs is a completely viable and oft-used option for collaborations, and you are welcome to encourage your students to create Google accounts and utilize the **Collaborations** feature using their personal Google accounts. To create a collaboration using Google Docs, follow the steps provided in this section and select **Google Docs** from the drop-down menu in step 3. Once you or your students authorize Google Docs access, the **Collaborations** feature will allow users to create a collaboration using Google Docs and it will function in the same way as described in the following steps.

To create a collaboration, complete these steps:

1. Click on the **Collaborations** tab of the left-hand side menu, as pictured at the bottom of the following screenshot:

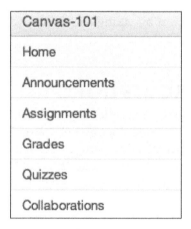

2. Canvas offers a nice explanation of collaborations and how to use them on the **Collaborations** page; so, take a second to read the text on the main **Collaborations** page. Then, click on the **Start a new collaboration** button above the text and to the right, as shown in this screenshot:

3. On the next page, you will see more explanation of collaborations; again, take the time to read this information to give yourself a better idea of how to use collaborations. The bottom half of the screen is labeled **Start a New Collaboration**. From the drop-down menu next to **Collaborate using**, select **EtherPad** as shown in the following screenshot:

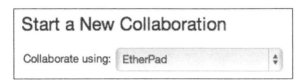

4. Next, enter the **Document name** and **Description** that you want students to see when they join the collaboration.

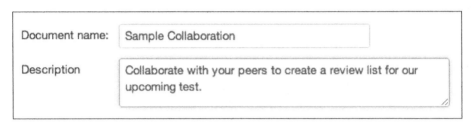

5. Below the description, you will see the option to select participants for the collaboration. You can select individual **People** to include, or you can select entire user **Groups** (which you would have previously set up from within the **People** tab on the left-hand side menu as discussed in *Chapter 3, Getting Ready to Launch Your Course*).

6. To select individual **People**, click on their names from the list of participants on the left-hand side. Their names will then appear on the right-hand side, and you can remove them by clicking the **X** that appears when you hover over their name. In the following screenshot, you see **Example Student** in the list of participants on the left-hand side and **John, Ryan** in the collaboration list on the right-hand side:

7. To select specific **Groups**, click on the **Groups** button above the participant list. You will see the list of groups that you previously created from within the **People** tab on the left-hand side menu, and you can select groups of people to include in the collaboration as pictured in the following screenshot:

8. When you have finished selecting participants or groups to include in the collaboration, click on the **Start Collaborating** button at the bottom of the screen, as shown in the following screenshot:

9. After that, the collaboration will be created and the EtherPad document will open in a new tab or window of your Internet browser. Close the EtherPad document and return to Canvas.

10. Your students will receive an invitation to join the collaboration you have created for them. Canvas EtherPad documents can be accessed at any time by clicking on the **Collaborations** tab on the left-hand side menu of the course.

Encourage your students to take advantage of the opportunity to work together using collaborations. The EtherPad document functions in much the same way as a basic word-processing document. In addition to basic formatting features, you can also use a timeslider to view the character-by-character progress of a document or generate an HTML code to embed the document elsewhere on the Web. These features appear on the top menu of the EtherPad page, and you can hover your mouse over each option for a description of the feature. Once a collaboration is created, the creator of the collaboration has the ability to edit or delete the collaboration.

Editing or deleting Collaborations

If you are the creator of a collaboration and you would like to edit or delete the collaboration, complete the following steps:

1. Click on the **Collaboration** tab on the left-hand side menu.

2. On the list of collaborations, find the collaboration you would like to edit or delete. To the right of the collaboration name, you will see the edit icon that looks like a pencil and the delete icon that looks like a trashcan. To edit the collaboration, click on the edit icon, as shown in the following screenshot:

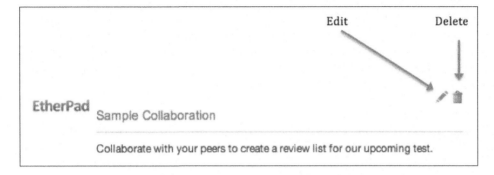

3. Within the **Collaborations** page, you will see the name and description of the collaboration turn into textboxes where you can make your changes. You also see the participant list appear, which you can adjust in the same way you did to create the collaboration. When you are finished editing the collaboration, click on **Update Collaboration** to save your changes.

4. To delete a collaboration, click on the delete icon. You will see a pop up asking if you really want to delete the collaboration—click on **Yes** and your collaboration will be deleted.

Providing opportunities for your students to work together and combine their ideas is a way of making the content they are engaging with more meaningful and personal. As content gains meaning for your students, that meaning will hopefully begin to impact their achievement positively. In order to assess student achievement, it is helpful for you to articulate your goals for students as they work through the content of your course; one such way to do so within Canvas is to use the **Outcomes** feature.

Setting up Outcomes

As general educational trends have moved toward more standardized and concrete methods of assessment in recent years, Canvas has incorporated the **Outcomes** feature to help you design assessment tools to keep up with the demands of teaching in the 21st century. The **Outcomes** feature of Canvas allows you to easily create, manage, and utilize assessment outcomes. Outcomes represent the skills, traits, or information you would like your students to come away with after your course. Standardized outcomes are becoming increasingly popular in North American schools and in institutions across the globe; many discipline-specific associations have created national standards that are comparable to the types of outcomes you would utilize in a Canvas course. Outcomes are also an excellent means of mapping your curriculum by providing you with a documentation of your learning goals. Should you choose to use your outcomes to create rubrics for assessment, you will also have a documentation of the ways in which your assessments directly relate to the concepts you set out to teach in the first place.

Once you have designed and created your outcomes, you will be able to quickly and easily access your outcomes when creating rubrics for assessments within your course. You can create outcomes that align to customized standards, benchmarks, and goals, or you can choose from common state and national standards that are already available through the **Outcomes** feature such as the Common Core Standards. Once you have set up your outcomes, you can use them to easily create a rubric for assignments, discussions, or quizzes within your course. The outcomes you create for one course are also accessible and usable within other courses; so, the hard work you put into creating outcomes for one course will come in handy if you would like to use them for another course you are teaching.

Creating Outcomes

To create a new outcome, we will perform the following steps:

1. Click on the **Outcomes** tab on the left-hand side menu of your course home page. You will see the **Learning Outcomes** page, with a menu across the top, a list of outcomes on the left-hand side (which will appear empty until you begin to add outcomes), and instructions in the center. These sections are labeled in the following screenshot:

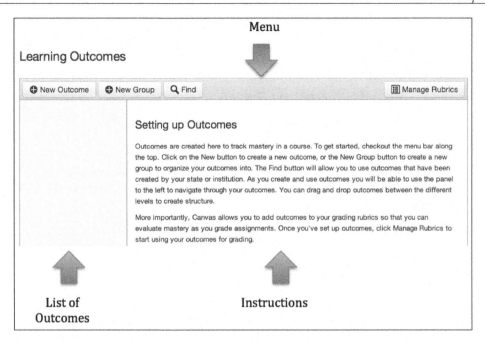

2. Take a look at the instructions, which offer an excellent overview of how you might choose to use outcomes within your course. Click on the **New Outcome** button in the top-left corner of the menu. You will see a new outcome template appear where the instructions were on the page.

3. Insert the desired name of your outcome into the **Name this outcome:** box at the top, then input the main body of your outcome in the **Describe this outcome:** Rich Content Editor box below. An example of a new outcome might be as follows:

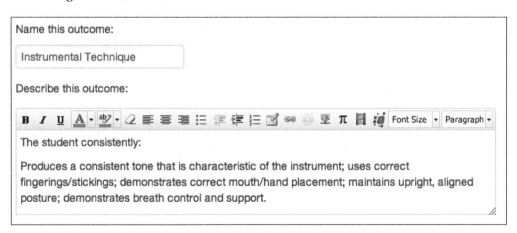

4. Once you are satisfied with the name and description of your outcome, look below the description at the **Criterion Ratings**. This section allows you to adjust how you wish to score your students' attainment of the outcome. The default criteria are as follows:

    ○ **Exceeds Expectations**: 5 points

    ○ **Meets Expectations**: 3 points

    ○ **Does Not Meet Expectations**: 0 points

5. To edit the **Criterion Ratings**, click on the edit icon that looks like a pencil at the bottom-right corner of each rating box, as shown in the following screenshot:

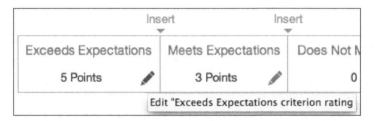

6. You will see the name of the criterion and the point value displayed in textboxes. You can then rename or modify the title of the criterion and adjust the point value. If you would like to, you can enter a longer description of what the student needs to do in order to achieve the criterion you are describing, rather than offering only a title for the criterion. This can clarify the expectations for students and can help them better understand how to meet each criterion. This idea will also be discussed further in the following sections regarding rubrics.

7. Click on the **OK** button at the bottom of the criterion box to save your criterion. You also have the option to delete the criterion by clicking on the **Delete** button at the bottom, as shown in the following screenshot:

8. If you would like to add more than three criteria for your outcome, click on the **Insert** arrow above the lines separating existing criteria as pictured in the following screenshot. This will create a new criterion that you can edit and save in the same way as the other criteria.

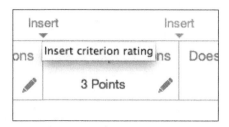

9. You can assign the minimum point value that students must receive to determine when students have reached a **Mastery** of the desired outcome. The following screenshot shows that students will have reached a **Mastery** of the outcome if they score a 3:

10. When you have finished creating your outcome, click on **Save** in the bottom-right corner of the page. You will see your outcome appear in the center of the screen where the instructions first appeared, and you will also see the **Delete Outcome** and **Edit Outcome** buttons show up underneath your new outcome. You are always able to edit or delete an outcome by selecting it from the list of outcomes and clicking on the edit or delete buttons that appear underneath the outcome.

Creating Outcome Groups

Once you have finished creating your first outcome, you might decide to create an **Outcome Group** to organize your outcomes. Examples of group labels might be by subject matter, grade level, or unit of study.

To create an **Outcome Group**, complete the following steps:

1. Click on the **New Group** button next to the **New Outcome** button on the top menu of the **Outcomes** page.

2. You will see a new outcome group template appear in the center of the screen with a box to name the group and a Rich Content Editor box to describe the group. This screen is very similar to the **New Outcome** template, but you will be describing the grouping of outcomes rather than the specific individual outcomes. The **New Group** template is shown in the following screenshot:

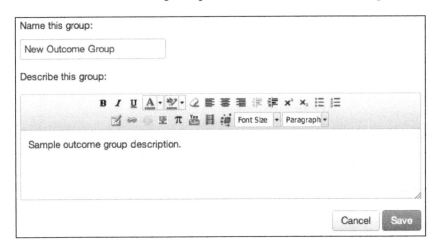

3. Click on **Save** at the bottom-right corner of the template. You will notice that your outcome group now appears to the left on the list of outcomes.

If you notice that your outcome groups and outcomes seem very disorganized on your screen, move around the screen erratically when you move your mouse, or are hard to click on, the Internet browser you are using might not be compatible with the way Canvas' outcomes are designed to work. Should you encounter this problem, try closing your Internet browser and logging in to Canvas using another browser. Common Internet browsers include Internet Explorer, Safari, Mozilla FireFox, Google Chrome, or Opera.

Now that you have created an outcome and an outcome group, you can add outcomes to your outcome groups:

1. To add an existing outcome to a newly created outcome group, click and hold on the title of the outcome in the list of outcomes and drag the outcome over the name of the desired outcome group. You will see a new column appear to the right of the list of outcomes that shows the outcome you moved nested within the outcome group.

2. To move the outcome back, simply click and drag the outcome back over to the main list of outcomes.

3. To add a new outcome to an outcome group, click on the outcome group from the list of outcomes. When the outcome group is selected, click the **New Outcome** button at the top and input the information for the new outcome as usual.

4. When you click on **Save**, the outcome will appear within the outcome group you selected, as seen in the following screenshot:

Finding existing Outcomes to use

As many institutions across North America and beyond have begun adopting national and state standards, Canvas has integrated the Common Core standards for English and Mathematics within the **Outcomes** feature for you to quickly and easily import into your Canvas course. The Common Core standards, which have been adopted by a large majority of the states in the United States, aim to make clear the outcomes desired for students at various grade levels.

To access and import the Common Core standards for use within your courses, complete the following steps:

1. Click on the **Find** button on the top menu of the **Outcomes** page.

2. In the pop-up window that appears, you will see an outcome group called **Common Core State Standards** listed on the left-hand side. If you click on this group, the **English Language Arts** and **Mathematics** outcome groups will appear in the column to the right, as displayed in the following screenshot:

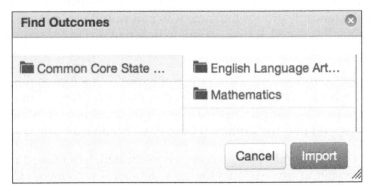

3. Notice that once you click on the **Common Core State Standards** outcome group, the **Import** button appears in the bottom-right corner of the window. You have the option to import everything within that group, or you can click through to more specific outcome groups such as specific grade levels of **English Language Arts** or **Mathematics**.

4. If you are an English or Mathematics teacher, it will be most helpful for you to click through those outcome groups and find the specific standards for your grade level. For example, if you are a 5th grade Math teacher, the selection in the following screenshot will allow you to import all of the Common Core State Standards for 5th grade Mathematics:

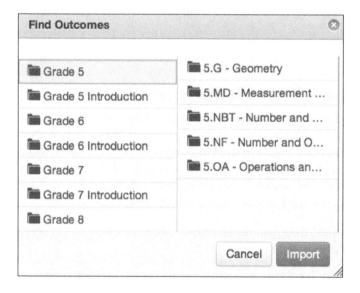

5. When you have selected the outcome group or specific outcome you would like to utilize in your Canvas course, click on the **Import** button and the selected items will appear in your **Outcomes** page.

6. Once the outcome groups appear on your **Outcomes** page, you can edit or delete the outcome groups the same way you would for an outcome group you manually created. It is important to note that you cannot edit the actual Common Core outcomes, as they are standardized in their wording and intent.

In addition to the Common Core standards, your specific institution might have standards or benchmarks that they have included in Canvas for you to access. Your institution's outcomes will appear in the far left of the **Find** pop-up window in the same place you would find the **Common Core State Standards** outcome group.

With all of our outcomes and outcome groups now created, let's move on to actually utilizing the outcomes to create rubrics for the assignments within your Canvas course.

Creating Rubrics and using Outcomes

The rubrics you can create within Canvas display the outcome followed by a grid containing the criterion ratings you created to rate students' performances. Using a rubric to assess a student's work, you will select the criterion rating that best describes the work they completed to meet the desired outcome. Based on the criterion ratings you choose and the point values associated with these ratings, Canvas determines the student's score based on the point value attained for each outcome.

With that understanding, let's look at how to create rubrics for Canvas assignments. Let's begin by creating a rubric within the **Outcomes** page using the following steps:

1. Click on the **Manage Rubrics** button at the top right of the **Outcomes** page menu, as shown in the following screenshot:

2. You will be taken to the **Course Rubrics** page. If you have not created any rubrics, this page will appear blank. On the right-hand side menu of this page, click on the **Add Rubric** button.

3. A new rubric template will appear on the **Course Rubrics** page. You can input a title for your rubric and then manually designate criteria and ratings below. For reference, the following screenshot shows the blank rubric template, and a description of how to manually add criteria and how ratings follow before we continue our discussion of using outcomes within the rubric (the phrase **Some Rubric** will appear as the default title of your rubric):

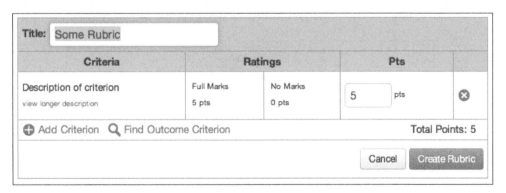

4. To change the title of your rubric, click on the textbox where **Some rubric** appears and type in the desired title.

5. To edit the description of the blank criterion, hover your mouse over the criterion box and click on the pencil-shaped edit icon that appears in the bottom-right corner of the box. The criterion box will change into a textbox where you can edit the description of the criterion. Note that creating a new criterion for a rubric is not the same as creating a new outcome; so, any new criteria you create will only be useable within the rubric for which they were created.

6. You can also edit the description by clicking on the view longer description link, which will open a pop-up window that allows you to edit the criterion description.

7. There are two ratings in the default template, **Full Marks** with 5 points and **No Marks** with 0 points. To edit these ratings, hover your mouse and click on the pencil-shaped edit icon that appears in the bottom-right corner of the box. In the following screenshot, you can see the edit icon in the bottom corner of the **Full Marks** box:

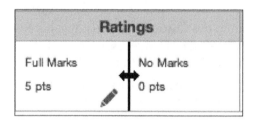

8. To add a new rating, click on the line between the two default ratings. You will see a new rating appear with the **Rating Description** title with 3 points; you will need to edit the title to reflect your desired description. You can add more ratings in the same fashion by clicking on the lines between ratings.

9. To add a new criterion, click on the **Add Criterion** button underneath the description of the first criterion. You will see a new criterion row appear in the rubric graph that you can edit and customize.

Now that we have covered how to manually input criteria and ratings into your rubric, let's return to our discussion on how to add **Outcomes** you created to your new rubric:

1. To include one of the outcomes you've created within your new rubric, click on the **Find Outcome Criterion** link next to the **Add Criterion** link at the bottom of your rubric. This will open a pop-up window that displays the outcome groups and outcomes you have already created or imported.

2. Locate the outcome you would like to use within your rubric by clicking through the outcome groups.

3. Click on the desired outcome, then click **Import** in the bottom-right corner of the pop-up window. Once you click on **Import**, the pop-up window will close and the selected outcome will appear within your rubric.

4. When you have adjusted all of the content within your rubric to your liking, click on the **Create Rubric** button in the bottom-right corner of the template. In the following screenshot, you will see a sample of the new template rubric completed with a title, a manually created criterion including an additional rating, and an imported outcome criterion:

Sample Rubric				
Criteria	**Ratings**			**Pts**
Sample Criterion 1	Full Marks 5 pts	Sample Rating 3 pts	No Marks 0 pts	5 pts
▦ Instrumental Technique view longer description threshold: 3 pts	Exceeds Expectations 5 pts	Meets Expectations 3 pts	Does Not Meet Expectations 0 pts	5 pts
			Total Points: 10	

Note that if you import an outcome into a rubric and then edit that outcome within the rubric, the outcome will remain unchanged in the outcome bank on the **Outcomes** page. When you import an outcome into a rubric, you are creating a copy of the outcome for use within the rubric rather than linking directly to the outcome.

Adding Rubrics to Assignments

With your first rubric now created, you can now add this rubric to an assignment as an assessment tool. To add a rubric to an assignment and use it for grading, complete the following steps:

1. Click on the **Assignments** link on the left-hand side menu of your course. From the list of assignments, click on the assignment to which you would like to add your rubric.

2. The selected assignment page will open, and at the bottom of the page, you will see a button that reads **Add Rubric** below the due date information for the assignment, as shown in the bottom-left corner of the following screenshot:

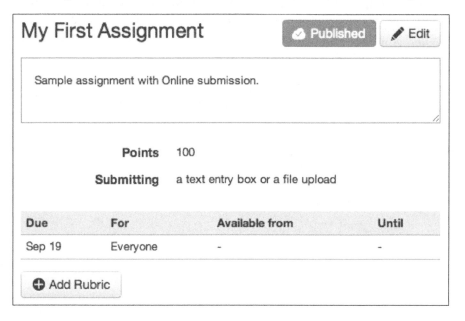

3. You will see a new rubric template appear below the assignment that includes the option to **Find a Rubric** at the top-right corner, as pictured in the following screenshot. You have the option to create a new rubric directly from this template, which will appear on the **Course Rubrics** page once you save it. However, if you wish to utilize the rubric you created previously, click on **Find a Rubric** to select the rubric from the list of course rubrics, as shown in the top-right corner of the following screenshot. A pop-up window will appear that will allow you to locate rubrics you have created within the course.

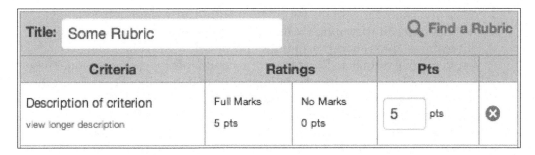

4. Once you find the rubric you would like to use for the assignment, select the rubric from the list and then click on the **Use This Rubric** button underneath the rubric, as pictured in the bottom-right corner of the following screenshot:

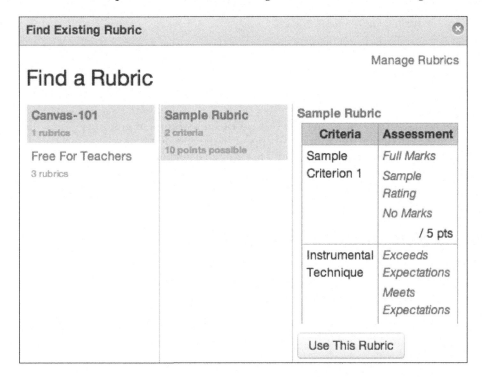

5. The pop-up window will close and you will see the rubric appear under the assignment description. If you would like to edit the rubric or adjust the settings for the rubric within the assignment, click on the pencil-shaped edit icon in the top-right corner of the rubric. Note that any changes you make to the rubric within the assignment will not adjust the rubric as it appears in the Course Rubrics list.

6. When you choose to edit the rubric from within an assignment, you have the option to edit the rubric for that assignment. In addition to the basic edit features, three checkbox options appear below the rubric that allow you to remove ratings to leave free-form comments for each criterion. These boxes also allow you to use the rating points to determine the grade for the assignment or to hide the total score for assessment results. Based on how you would like to use the rubric within your course and for the chosen assignment, you may decide to check any of these options to enable you to leave more specific feedback when assessing your students or simplify grading with points. Click on **Update Rubric** when you have selected the desired options, as shown in the following screenshot:

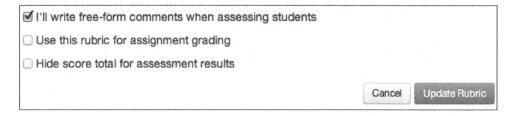

 If you check the **Use this rubric for assignment grading** option, the rubric will appear in the SpeedGrader when you grade the assignment. This is often a goal of creating a rubric in the first place, so make sure that you check this box if you wish to use the rubric for grading purposes.

Using Rubrics for Assessment

Once you have set up the rubric for the assignment, you can actually use the rubric for assessment and grading purposes. To do so, you will need to open the SpeedGrader for the assignment:

1. Scroll up on the assignment page and click on the SpeedGrader link on the right-hand side menu. This will open SpeedGrader and you will be able to see a student's submissions for the selected assignment.

2. On the right-hand side of SpeedGrader, you will now see an option that says **View Rubric** in the **Assessment** section at the top, as shown in the following screenshot:

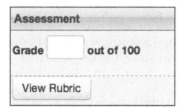

3. If you click on this button, the rubric will appear in a pop-up window and you can offer the student feedback on their submission using the rubric. You can click on the options listed under **Ratings** to assign points, manually assign rating point scores for each criterion, or leave comments if you selected the free-form comment option.

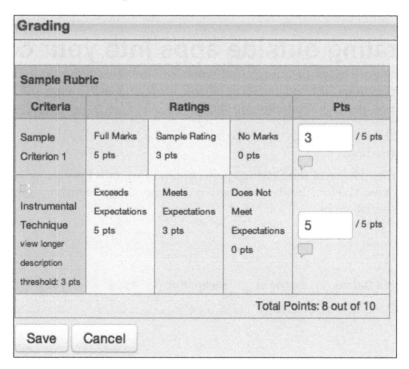

4. Click on the **Save** button at the bottom when you are finished grading with the rubric. You will see the completed rubric now appears on the right-hand side of the SpeedGrader below the **Assessment** section. The student will be able to see this completed rubric as assignment feedback and gauge how they did on the assignment based on the criteria and ratings.

5. When you have finished grading the assignment completely, you can click through to other submissions using the arrows next to the student's name at the top as usual.

6. Outcomes and rubrics offer you a wide range of opportunities to clarify and standardize expectations while personalizing and specifying feedback for each student in your course. As a learning tool, outcomes and rubrics can push your students to think differently about how to complete assignments for your course and improve students' overall performance.

Another feature of Canvas that can improve overall performance, both for you and your students, is the use of outside apps that you can integrate into your course.

Integrating outside apps into your course

Canvas has partnered with a number of online resources to allow you to integrate outside applications (abbreviated as apps) into your courses. To view the list of available apps, perform the following steps:

1. Click on the **Settings** tab at the bottom of the left-hand side menu on your course home page.

2. Across the top of the **Settings** page, you will see tabs for various settings and options. The fourth tab, as shown in the following screenshot, is the **Apps** tab—click on it:

3. When you open the **Apps** tab, you will see brief instructions at the top of the page with a large list of available apps displayed below, as pictured in the following screenshot:

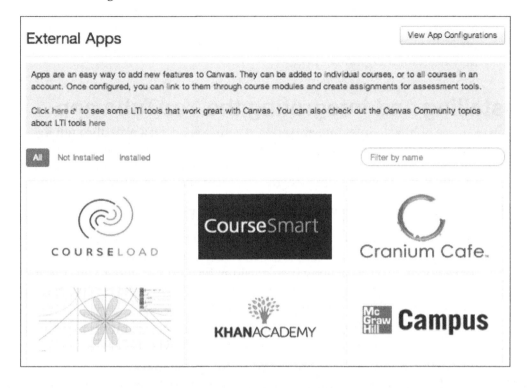

4. Take some time to scroll through the available apps to find options that you might wish to integrate into your course. If you hover your mouse over the icon for an app, a description will appear over the icon that will explain what integrating that app will allow you to do. For example, if you use a McGraw-Hill textbook in your course, check to see whether the textbook has any interactive online resources listed; if it does, you can integrate the McGraw-Hill app directly into your course so that your students can take advantage of the online resources directly through Canvas. You might wish to connect the **Khan Academy** app to your course to open the door for your students to explore the myriad of free learning resources offered by Khan Academy. If you know you are going to be using lots of videos during your course, consider integrating the **YouTube** and **Vimeo** apps to more easily access and embed content from these sites into your course. Select the app you would like to integrate into your course by clicking on the app icon on the main list.

5. On the app page that opens, click **Add Tool** underneath the icon and then follow any on-screen instructions that appear. Once you have followed all the instructions, the app will be integrated into your course. You may need to obtain additional information from your institution for certain apps, such as apps that require payment or access codes to use. Check in with your institution's IT or administrative team to obtain additional information you may need for integrating apps.

Installing and integrating the YouTube app

As an example of how to integrate an app into your course, let's walk through the steps of installing the YouTube app for your course. Each app will function slightly differently after you have installed it into your course, but the following section will show you exactly how to install and use the YouTube app as an example.

To install the YouTube app, complete the following steps:

1. From the list of available apps, scroll down and find the **YouTube** app. Hover your mouse over the app to see a description of what the app will allow you to do. You will see that installing the app will add a YouTube icon to your Rich Content Editor that will allow you to search for and embed videos from YouTube directly in to Canvas.

2. Click on the **YouTube** app. You will see a page open with more details about the YouTube app and what it will allow you to do within Canvas.

3. To install the app, click the blue **+ Add Tool** button that appears directly below the YouTube logo on the left-hand side, as pictured in the following screenshot:

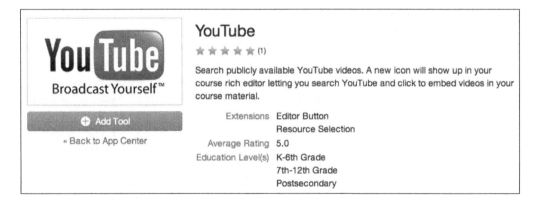

4. When you click on the **+ Add Tool** button, the installation will begin automatically. You will see a pop-up window appear momentarily with the name of the app that will close after Canvas has finished saving the name of the app. The app page will display an icon indicating that the installation is loading, and then **YouTube** will appear on your list of installed apps. As displayed in the following screenshot, your list will only include one app once you have finished installing **YouTube**:

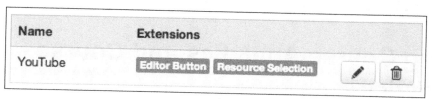

5. When your installation has finished, you will be able to utilize the YouTube icon that will appear within the Rich Content Editor when you post or edit content including assignments, content pages, discussion posts, and announcements. You will also be able to insert YouTube videos directly into course modules after integrating the app. To use the app within the Rich Content Editor, click on the YouTube icon as highlighted in the following screenshot:

6. When you click on the YouTube icon in the Rich Content Editor, a pop-up window will appear with a search bar that allows you to search for videos on YouTube. Type in your search terms and then click on **Search**.

7. From the results that appear, click on the name of the video you would like to embed and the pop-up window will close. The selected video will appear within the Rich Content Editor textbox and will be playable once you save the item you are editing such as a discussion post, assignment, or content page.

By utilizing the wide variety of apps available to you for installation and integration within your Canvas account, you have the opportunity to create an engaging, unique, and transformative learning experience for your students online. With the combination of your teaching expertise, clearly articulated outcomes incorporated into rubrics, and the integration of cutting-edge apps, you have the tools to increase student engagement and achievement. Rather than assuming that this statement is true, let's take a look at the tracking tools Canvas has to offer for you to track student activity, engagement, and growth.

Using Course Analytics and Course Statistics

Canvas allows you to easily view how users are participating within your course, when most assignments are being submitted, and how a class is doing as a whole based on a combination of individual grades. In addition, Canvas allows you to easily view specific elements that make up your course such as the number of items within your course or how much file storage space your course takes up. To begin, let's check out how to view activity and achievement within your course using the **Course Analytics** feature.

Viewing Course Analytics

To view the course analytics, complete the following steps:

1. On the home page of your course, look at the right-hand side menu. Click on the **View Course Analytics** button, which is the fifth option down in the following screenshot:

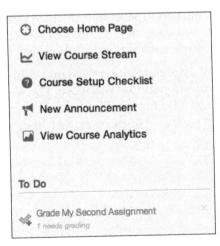

2. Once you click on the **View Course Analytics** button, you will see the **Course Analytics** page. This page contains three main sections that include explanations and graphs: **Activity**, **Assignments**, and **Grades**.

As your course progresses while students interact with the course content, submit assignments, and receive grades, your course analytics will grow and change to indicate the evolution of your course from start to finish. The following screenshot offers an example of what your course might look like after two months of use:

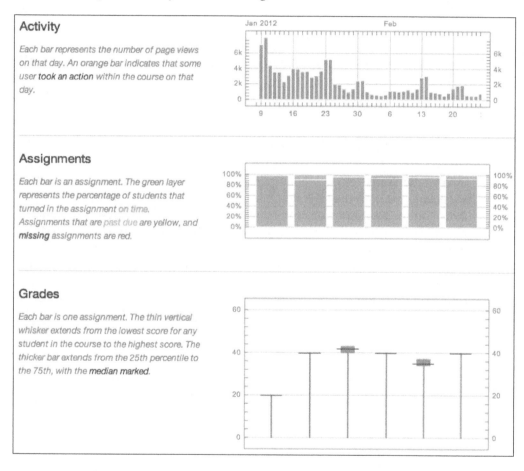

The explanations underneath each section heading help you to understand the graphs that appear to the right, and the graphs offer visual representation of the movement within your course. While the **Course Analytics** feature allows you to track aspects of the interactions with content happening in your course, the **Course Statistics** feature lets you quickly and easily view a breakdown of what makes up your course.

Viewing Course Statistics

To view **Course Statistics** for your course, follow these steps:

1. Click on the **Settings** link on the left-hand side menu of your course.

2. Once the **Settings** page is open, look at the right-hand side menu. Click on the **Course Statistics** button, which appears as the second option in the following screenshot:

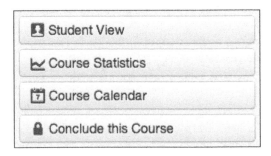

3. The **Course Statistics** page will open and you will be able to view the statistics by clicking through the tabs along the top of the page. The **Totals** tab will show you the total number of items within your course. The **Assignments** tab will show you how many assignments of each type you have created and how many submissions have been made for each of those assignments. The **Students** tab will show you students who have recently logged in and their activity while logged in. The **File Storage** tab will show you how many files you have uploaded to your course and how much storage space those files are using up. The following screenshot displays the content of the **Totals** tab with the other tabs visible along the top:

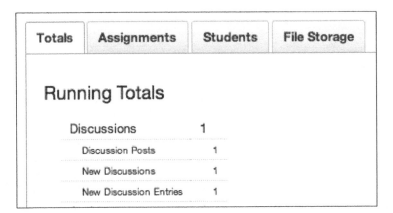

As users interact with your course, both the analytics and statistics features of Canvas will become more and more useful. You will be able to see what items in your course students most frequently utilize, which can help you in adjusting the types of content you choose to include in your course and in designing your next course.

Summary

In this chapter, we began by discussing how to navigate and use the Canvas mobile app with your mobile devices. The following section covered the **Collaborations** feature of Canvas, including the use of EtherPad and Google Docs. Next, we covered the **Outcomes** feature of Canvas, including how to create individual outcomes as well as how to organize those outcomes into outcome groups. We also covered how to find and import the Common Core standards for use within your courses. After that, we learned how to incorporate outcomes into **Rubrics** to use as assessment tools for grading assignments in your course. Then, we moved on to installing external **Apps** for integration into your course, using the YouTube app as an example. Finally, we examined how **Course Analytics** and **Course Statistics** can help you monitor activity and achievement within your course and improve engagement for the future.

At this point, we have covered all of the basics of Canvas course design. As we move into the next chapter, we will cover the options you have to find help with questions or problems you might encounter while using Canvas. We will look specifically at the range of options found within Canvas as well as help options available to you outside of Canvas.

6
Where to Go for Help

As you work through building and teaching your Canvas course, you are bound to run into questions or concerns about your course. In some instances, you might encounter error messages, broken links, or other problems within your course. Fortunately, Canvas has a vast number of built-in resources that you can utilize to help solve your problems. In addition, there are other resources available online or through your institution that can help you solve problems and answer questions you might encounter. In this chapter, we will discuss a number of options you have, both built into Canvas or available elsewhere, to obtain help with Canvas should you run into trouble. Topics covered in this chapter include the following:

- Searching and using the Canvas Guides
- Reporting a problem with Canvas
- Obtaining pricing information for the use of Canvas at your institution
- Requesting a new feature for Canvas
- Finding help from your institution's tech support team

To begin, let's start with the help options Canvas offers from within the site.

Finding help within Canvas

There are two **Help** links that are visible in most areas of Canvas. The first is in the top-right menu of your screen on the far right, as shown in the following screenshot:

The second link is on the bottom menu on the far left of your screen, as shown in the following screenshot:

BY INSTRUCTURE   Help | Privacy policy | Terms of service | Facebook | Twitter

These menus are visible on the vast majority of pages within Canvas, with the exception of certain pages such as **SpeedGrader**. The ease of access to support within Canvas allows you and your students to troubleshoot and solve your own problems quickly and easily. Clicking on either of these links will open the **Help** pop-up window for Canvas, which provides you with the options pictured in the following screenshot:

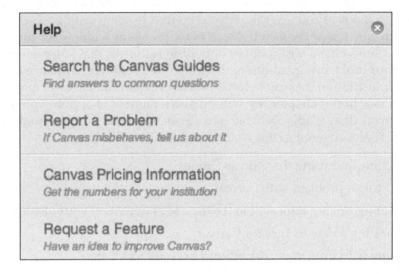

The first option, **Search the Canvas Guides**, brings you to the hub of Canvas' online support resources. Let's begin by exploring the **Canvas Guides** within the **Help Center** and learning how to find what you need within this support resource.

Exploring the Canvas Guides and Community Forums

If you need help with Canvas, you can either browse or search the **Canvas Guides**, or you can ask the **Canvas Community** for help. To begin, let's examine how to browse and search the **Canvas Guides** for the information you need.

Browsing and searching the Canvas Guides

The **Canvas Guides** offer you a huge number of user manuals and instructions. Compared to other websites, the layout of the **Canvas Guides** closely resembles a **Frequently Asked Questions (FAQs)** format, wherein you are able to browse or search for the question or problem you are facing, and then click on the question to see the answer. When you click on **Search the Canvas Guides** in the **Help** pop-up window, you are brought to the **Canvas Guides** page, pictured in the following screenshot, which lists a number of guidance pages that are constantly updated by the Canvas operating team.

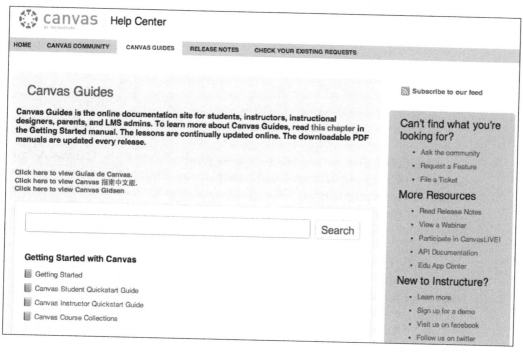

From the main **Canvas Guides** page, you can search for a question or for the feature with which you are having trouble. In addition, you can browse through multiple guides within the headings described as follows:

- **Getting Started with Canvas**: This section offers you four guides to view: the **Getting Started** manual, the **Canvas Student Quickstart Guide**, the **Canvas Instructor Quickstart Guide**, and the **Canvas Course Collections**. Clicking on any of these guides will display a number of further subsections that include questions you might encounter and tutorial lessons that you might find helpful in mastering the use of Canvas or troubleshooting problems you are encountering. This section features a general overview in the first guide, and then allows users to view questions that will apply to them based on the user role they fulfill within a course. The **Canvas Course Collections** page offers you a number of public Canvas courses that you can view as examples of what you can do within Canvas. The **Getting Started** options are pictured in the following screenshot:

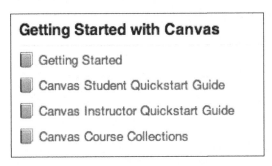

- **Canvas Guides**: This section offers you six guides to view: the **Canvas Admin Guide**, the **Canvas Instructor Guide**, the **Canvas Student Guide**, the **Canvas Observer Guide**, the **Canvas Designer Guide**, and the **Canvas Video Guide**. Recall that each user in your Canvas course participates as a specific user type—these guides address many of the user types we discussed in *Chapter 3, Getting Ready to Launch Your Course*. The guidance for users enrolled as a **TA** can be found within the guide for **Designers**, and the guide for an **Administrator** (**Admin**) presents detailed technical information that would be helpful for individuals working for an institutional IT department. The Admin guide might also be useful to you if you wish to explore some of the advanced features of Canvas that are not covered here. You can direct your students to the Student guide as a way to help them acclimate to using Canvas. The **Canvas Video Guide** offers you video tutorials for a huge variety of tasks you might undertake while using Canvas. These videos are tremendously helpful, so take some time to look through the options available to you on this page. The **Canvas Guides** menu is pictured in the following screenshot:

Canvas Guides

- Canvas Admin Guide
- Canvas Instructor Guide
- Canvas Student Guide
- Canvas Observer Guide
- Canvas Designer Guide
- Canvas Video Guide

- **Mobile Guides – Canvas by Instructure**: This section offers you manuals for help within versions of the Canvas mobile app for Android and iOS phones and tablets.

- **Mobile guides - MagicMarker**: This section provides help with the iOS MagicMarker tablet app.

- **Mobile Guides – Polls for Canvas**: This section offers you manuals for help within versions of the Poll mobile app for Android and iOS phones and tablets.

- **Mobile Guides – SpeedGrader**: This guide provides information and support for the SpeedGrader mobile app for iOS tablet devices. The following screenshot displays the menus for each of the **Mobile Guides** menus:

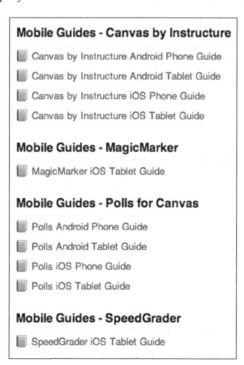

Mobile Guides - Canvas by Instructure

- Canvas by Instructure Android Phone Guide
- Canvas by Instructure Android Tablet Guide
- Canvas by Instructure iOS Phone Guide
- Canvas by Instructure iOS Tablet Guide

Mobile Guides - MagicMarker

- MagicMarker iOS Tablet Guide

Mobile Guides - Polls for Canvas

- Polls Android Phone Guide
- Polls Android Tablet Guide
- Polls iOS Phone Guide
- Polls iOS Tablet Guide

Mobile Guides - SpeedGrader

- SpeedGrader iOS Tablet Guide

As you browse through each of these headings, you will be able to read through dozens of up-to-date pages that show you exactly how to accomplish certain tasks, complete with step-by-step screenshots and quite often accompanying video tutorials. While you have already learned much of the information covered in many of the tutorials from the first five chapters of this book, the **Canvas Guides** serve as an easily accessible and constantly updated resource for you as you experiment and increase your knowledge of Canvas.

Searching the Canvas Guides

While browsing the Canvas Guides can be very helpful, you also have the option to search the **Canvas Guides** by entering search terms into the search bar on the main Canvas Guides page.

To search the **Canvas Guides**, complete the following steps:

1. Open the main **Canvas Guides** page and click on the **Search** bar that appears above the list of Canvas Guide headings, as indicated in the following screenshot:

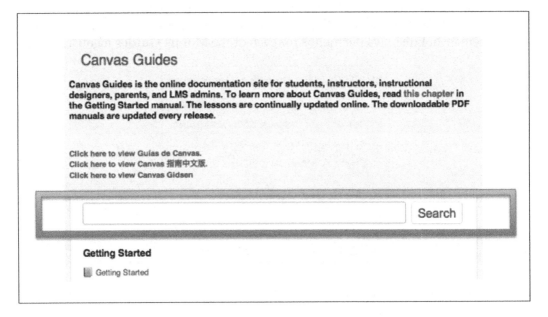

2. Type in your question or search terms, and then click on the **Search** button as shown to the right in the following screenshot:

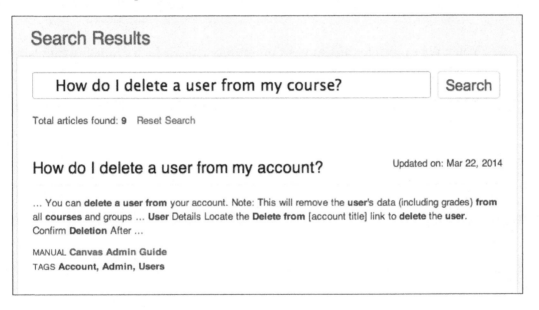

How do I delete a user from my course? | Search

3. You will be taken to the search results page, where you will be able to browse through the **Canvas Guides** topics that might pertain to your question based on the words included in your search. You can browse through the search results to find the article that will best address your question. The following screenshot shows you a results page, indicating that nine articles might address the question entered:

Search Results

How do I delete a user from my course? | Search

Total articles found: **9**   Reset Search

How do I delete a user from my account?   Updated on: Mar 22, 2014

... You can **delete a user from** your account. Note: This will remove the **user's** data (including grades) **from** all **courses** and groups ... **User** Details Locate the **Delete from** [account title] link to **delete** the **user**. Confirm **Deletion** After ...

MANUAL **Canvas Admin Guide**
TAGS **Account, Admin, Users**

4. When you find the article that seems to address your question, click on the bold title of the article. You will be taken to the article page where you can find instructions and guidance to address your question.

The **Canvas Guides** are an excellent place to find answers to questions that might arise as you are creating, designing, or teaching your course. However, you might not always be able to find the answer to your question within the existing **Canvas Guides**. If you are unable to locate an answer to a question that arises, you can visit the **Community Forums** and post specific questions that other members of the Canvas community can answer.

Asking questions in the Community Forums

There are two easy ways to access the Canvas **Community Forums**, where you can browse and search for answers to questions that other users have posed:

1. The first link can be found on the top menu of the **Canvas Guides** page. Click on the **Canvas Community** tab of the top menu, as indicated in the following screenshot:

2. You will be taken to the **Canvas Community** page, which displays a number of forums that you can browse through. To find the forum in which you can ask a question to the community, click on either the **Higher Education** or **K12** forum under the list of **Community Forums**, depending on which forum applies to the audience of your course. These forums are shown on the right-hand column in the following screenshot:

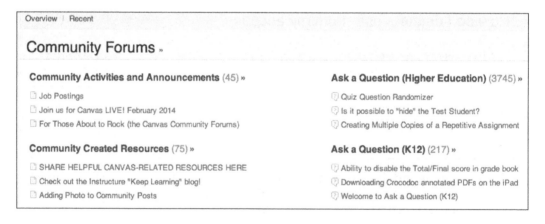

3. You can also access the **Community Forums** by clicking on the link at the top of the right-hand side menu on the **Canvas Guides** page.

4. Look to the right-hand side of the **Canvas Guides** page. At the top, you will see a heading that reads **Can't find what you're looking for?**. Go ahead and click on the first link, **Ask the community**, as pictured in the following screenshot:

Can't find what you're looking for?

- Ask the community
- Request a Feature
- File a Ticket

5. You will be taken to the **Ask a Question (Higher Education)** forum, where you are able to browse and ask questions related to higher education Canvas courses. Should you wish to view the K-12 forum, you should click on the **Canvas Community** tab on the top menu and access the forum as described in the preceding section.

6. Once you have navigated to the appropriate community forum, you can search the forum for your question by typing your question into the search bar at the top of the page.

7. You can also browse questions that have already been asked and answered by filtering the questions displayed by **Most asked, Recent, Needs Answer**, or **Answered**. The following screenshot indicates the search bar and filter options you can use to navigate the **Community Forums**:

If you are unable to find your question within the **Community Forums**, you can choose to ask a question and post it to the forums for other users to answer. To post a question on the Community Forums, complete the following steps:

1. Click on the **Ask a Question** button on the right-hand side next to the filter options, as shown in the bottom-right corner of the following screenshot:

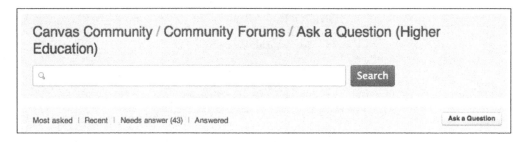

2. A page will open that will allow you to ask your question and describe what you are encountering. You will notice when you type your question that related topics appear below your question that might be able to answer your question. If none of the related topics meet your needs, proceed to describe what you are encountering in the main textbox. The following screenshot offers a sample of a question that could be posted:

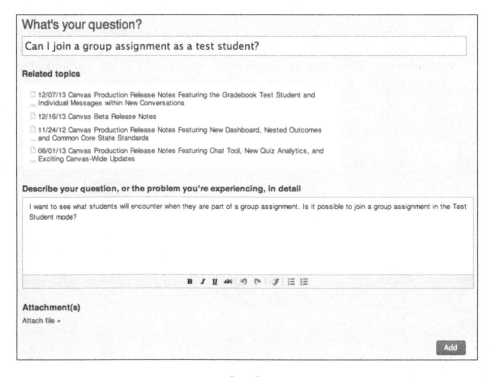

3. You can format the text of your response using the editing buttons underneath the main text box. These options function the same way as the options in the Rich Content Editor found elsewhere in Canvas.

4. You can also attach a file to your question. You might consider attaching a screenshot or another useful file if it will help other users understand what you are encountering.

5. When you have finished typing your question, click on the **Add** button in the bottom-right corner of the screen. Your question will be added to the **Community Forums** and other users will be able to see and respond to your question.

Once your question is posted to the community forum, you will be able to see when another Canvas user has posted a reply and the status of your question changes to **Answered**. Depending on your notification settings, you might receive an e-mail notifying you that another user has responded to your post. While we're in the **Community Forums**, let's discuss how to respond to questions other users have posted.

Responding to questions in the Community Forums

The **Community Forums** work well when everyone combines their knowledge to help one another out in confusing situations, so if you see a question that you know how to answer or that reflects one of your own questions, go ahead and help out the community by responding to that question.

To respond to a question in the **Community Forums**, complete the following steps:

1. Navigate to the **Community Forums** in the same way you would to browse questions or ask your own question. Select the **Needs answer** filter to view questions that you might be able to answer. This option is underlined in the following screenshot:

Most asked | Recent | Needs answer (43) | Answered   Ask a Question

2. Once you can see the posted questions that still need answers, locate the question that you would like to respond to. Your response might be an answer, or you might wish to let Canvas know that you have the same question. Click on the bold question title, as highlighted in the following screenshot. The question page will open, displaying the question heading at the top, the main body of the question below, and any responses that other users have posted in the **Comments** section below the question.

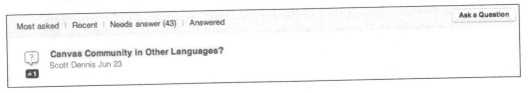

3. One of the options you have in the **Community Forums** is to tell the community that you would also like to know the answer to a question; you could think of it as clicking on *Like* on a post on Facebook or clicking on *Favorite* for a tweet on Twitter. Underneath the main body of the question, you will see a button that reads **Be the first!** to indicate that you would also like the question answered, as pictured in the following screenshot:

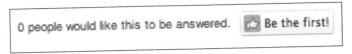

4. Alternatively, this option might appear as **Me too!** if other users have already expressed interest in knowing the answer to the question, as pictured in the following screenshot. Click on one of these buttons to flag the question and let the community know that multiple users have the same question:

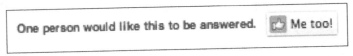

5. If you would like to post a comment on the question to answer the question, share similar feedback, or respond to other users' comments, scroll down on the page to the **Add a comment** textbox underneath the **Comments** section.

6. The **Add a comment** text box is the same style as the text box we discussed to post a question to the **Community Forums**. You can type your comment into the text box, adjust the formatting using the options underneath the text box, and attach a file using the button on the bottom-left side.

7. When your comment is complete, click on the **Save Comment** button at the bottom right and your comment will be posted publicly for other users to see. The following screenshot offers you a sample comment response:

The **Canvas Guides** and the **Community Forums** offer you a huge wealth of knowledge regarding Canvas. By browsing and searching these resources, you will most likely be able to figure out how to accomplish certain tasks and find answers to questions you encounter. However, you might encounter circumstances where Canvas is malfunctioning, or as described in the **Help** menu, if Canvas misbehaves.

Reporting a problem

While designing, building, or teaching your course, you might run into features that are flat out not working. Usually, you will be able to tell if something is not working by an error message appearing at the top of your screen or displaying on the page you are trying to view. Should you encounter an error message, the message might include a link to report the problem. If not, you can tell Canvas about the issue through the **Help** menu. To report a problem, complete the following steps:

1. Click on the **Help** link on the top-right menu or the bottom menu of Canvas.
2. From the pop-up **Help** menu, click on **Report a Problem**, which appears as the second option in the following screenshot:

3. This will open a dialogue window that allows you to input the subject, description, and priority of your problem. You will notice at the top of the window that you are submitting a ticket for a personal response from a member of the Canvas support team. Also notice that the dialogue window includes a link to the **Canvas Guides** as a reminder to check the **Canvas Guides** and **Community Forums** first before submitting a ticket. This helps reduce redundant help requests, which in turn allows the Canvas support team to respond to your problems more quickly. The dialogue window to report a problem is pictured in the following screenshot:

4. You can enter the subject of your problem, which will offer the support team member an instant idea of what you're encountering, and then you can enter a detailed description of the problem.

When entering a description, make sure that you include each step you went through before encountering the problem. For example, if you encounter an error message every time you try to view a custom content page, describe how you are navigating to the page and exactly what is displayed each time you receive the error message.

5. Above the **Description** textbox, you will see a message requesting that you include a link for a screencast or screenshot that will show the support team member exactly what you're encountering. You can follow the suggested link to download the **Jing** software that will allow you to create a video screencast for free. Look ahead to the following section if you would like to include a screencast using Jing.

6. When you have finished typing the description of your problem, click on the drop-down menu underneath the question **How is this affecting you?** to select the priority of your question. From the options that are displayed, you will notice the user-friendly language that helps you gauge the importance of your problem in order to report it to the Canvas support team. You will see a number of options, as shown in the following screenshot:

How is this affecting you?

✓ Please select one...
Just a casual question, comment, idea, suggestion
I need some help but it's not urgent
Something's broken but I can work around it for now
I can't get things done until I hear back from you
EXTREME CRITICAL EMERGENCY!!

The options are described in the following bullet points:

- **Just a casual question, comment, idea, suggestion**: Select this option if your message refers to something that is not directly impeding the building or teaching of your course. This marks your message as the lowest priority for an immediate response; however, the Canvas support team is generally very prompt in replying to even the lowest priority messages.

- **I need some help but it's not urgent**: Select this option if you are having a problem with Canvas but it is not directly impeding the building or teaching of your course. This marks your message as the second lowest priority for an immediate response.

- **Something's broken but I can work around it for now**: Select this option if the problem you are encountering needs to be solved in the future but is not immediately preventing you from building or teaching your course. This marks your message as the middle priority for an immediate response.

○ **I can't get things done until I hear back from you**: Select this option if the problem you are encountering is directly impeding you from building or teaching your course. This marks your message as the second highest priority for an immediate response.

○ **EXTREME CRITICAL EMERGENCY!!**: Select this option if the problem you are encountering is directly impeding you from building or teaching your course and it is having a significant impact on the success of the participants in your course. This marks your message as the highest priority for an immediate response and should be used only in extreme cases.

7. After you have entered the subject, description, and selected a priority from the **How is this affecting you?** drop-down menu, click on the **Submit Ticket** button at the bottom of the pop-up window.

8. Again, if you would like to create and link to a screencast or screenshot using Jing to include in your description of the problem, please refer to the following section before submitting your ticket.

9. Once you have submitted your help ticket, you will receive a confirmation email that it has been received and a member of the support team will follow up with you personally to help you resolve the problem.

Creating a screencast using Jing

As mentioned in the preceding section, you can record a screencast or a screenshot using Jing. Jing is a program that you can download for free and allows you to record a video of your computer screen that shows exactly what your screen looks like when you encounter the problem you are reporting. Please note that the following installation and usage procedures are described based on their use with a Mac and might be slightly different for PC users. Note that the screenshots in this section are taken from a Mac computer.

There are a number of screencast and screenshot programs available for free and for purchase online. This section only discusses Jing as the Canvas-recommended software, but you are free to use other programs to record and attach your screencasts or screenshots.

To download Jing and create a screencast or screenshot to include in your help ticket, complete the following steps.

1. Click on the link to Jing that is included in the **Report a Problem** pop-up window, as shown in the following screenshot:

Description
Include a link to a screencast/screenshot using something like Jing.

2. Make sure that you leave the **Report a Problem** pop-up window open in your browser, as you will return to the window at the end of this process where you need to paste the link to your screencast in the description of your problem. At this point, open a new tab or window in Canvas in your browser so that you can recreate the problem you are encountering when you record your screencast. After you have opened the new window of Canvas, return to the **Report a Problem** pop up and click on the link to Jing. You will be taken to this website: `http://www.techsmith.com/download/jing/`.

3. On the Jing website, click on the download button that corresponds to the operating system you are using.

4. Follow the standard installation procedures for your operating system to install Jing onto your computer.

5. Once Jing is installed, open the program. You will see a video tutorial appear; go ahead and take a few minutes to watch the video tutorial to gain a better understanding of how Jing works and what you can do with it.

6. After you have watched the tutorial video, click on the **Get Started** button under the tutorial video. You will be prompted to create a Jing account by entering your contact information and following the onscreen instructions to create your account.

7. When you have successfully created your account, Jing will open. When the program is running, you will see a faint yellow circle in the top-right corner of your screen. Hover your mouse over the circle to see the three options that appear: **Capture**, **History**, and **More**. Click on the **Capture** option, as displayed in the following screenshot:

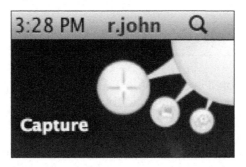

8. When you click on **Capture**, you will be able to select which part of your screen you would like to include in the screen capture.

9. To record a screencast or screenshot of the problem you are encountering in Canvas, click on your browser window with the Canvas page open that you would like to record. You will notice that the outside regions of your screen are grayed out and will not be included in the screen capture.

10. Once you have selected the capture area, you will see a menu appear with four icons that allow you to **Capture an Image**, **Capture a Video**, **Redo Selection**, or **Cancel** your capture.

11. To record a screencast, select the second icon, **Capture a Video**. A window will appear asking which microphone you wish to use. If you wish to record audio narration as you click through the problem you are encountering and recording on your screen, select the microphone you wish to use.

12. Once you have selected your audio options, you will see a large countdown starting at **3**, which appears over the section of your screen that will be recorded in the video. When the countdown is finished, your recording will begin automatically.

13. When the recording starts, you will see a menu appear in the bottom-left corner of your screen with five buttons: a **Finish** icon that looks like a stop button, a **Pause** button, a **Mute** button to turn off your microphone, a **Reset** button, and a **Cancel** button. These options are indicated as the **Recording Menu** in the following screenshot:

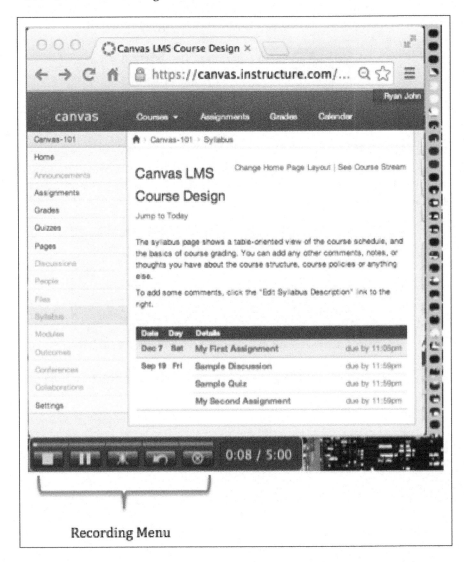

Recording Menu

14. As the recording begins, you can navigate through the problem you are encountering in Canvas. As you click through each step, narrate your actions if you have enabled your microphone. Click on the **Mute** button if you would not like to include narration.

15. When you have finished recording the issue, click on the **Finish** button that looks like a square. A new menu will appear underneath the preview of your recording. Watch your recording to make sure it includes everything you would like. If you are finished, enter a name for your video and click on the **Share via Screencast.com** button. You can also **Save** the video to your computer or **Cancel** the recording. The **Share via Screencast.com** button is visible in the bottom-left corner of the following screenshot:

16. Your video will automatically begin to upload to http://screencast.com. A notification window will appear once your upload is complete and you can follow the link in the window to view your video online, as pictured in the following screenshot:

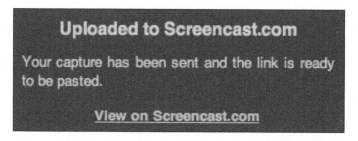

17. Once you can see the video in your browser, copy the link to your video from the web address bar.

18. Return to your **Report a Problem** pop-up window in Canvas. Paste the link to your recording in the **Description** section of your problem, finish creating your help ticket as described in the previous section, and then click on **Submit Ticket**.

Now that we have covered how to **Report a Problem**, let's take a look at obtaining Canvas pricing information for your institution.

Obtaining Canvas pricing information

If you are using the Free for Teachers version of Canvas, chances are that the institution you work for has not adopted Canvas as its learning management system. As you gain more familiarity with Canvas, you might decide that Canvas would be an excellent choice for your institution to adopt. You may or may not see the option **Canvas Pricing Information** on your help menu depending on the way your version of Canvas is configured. The following section will guide you through this option if it is available to you.

To obtain pricing information about Canvas, complete the following steps:

1. Open the **Help** menu by clicking on the link in the top-right or bottom menus, and then select the **Canvas Pricing Information** option, as pictured in the following screenshot. A new tab or window will open in your browser that takes you to the Canvas website.

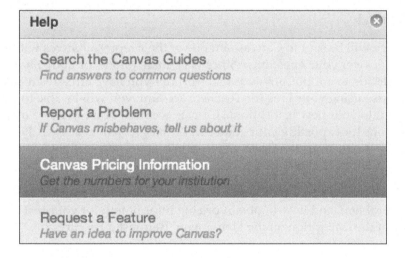

2. At the bottom-right corner of your screen, you will see a tab that reads **Have a question?** that stays visible no matter where you scroll on the page. Click on this tab.

3. This tab will expand into a message box that allows you to send a message to Canvas, requesting information about the pricing of Canvas for your institution. Go ahead and fill in the following information:

   ° Name

   ° E-mail address

   ° Institution or organization

   ° Your title

   ° The subject of your message

   ° The body of your message, explaining your specific situation and the nature of the information you would like to receive

   ° Your phone number if you would like to discuss pricing over the phone.

4. From there, click on the **Leave a Message** button at the bottom-left corner of the tab.

Your message will be sent to Canvas and one of their representatives will be in touch with you to answer your questions, either via e-mail, phone, or both. Should your institution decide to adopt Canvas as its LMS after you have already created and taught a course using your Free for Teachers account, you will be able to roll your course over into your new institutional Canvas account. You can do so by following the instructions for exporting your course in *Chapter 7, Now You're Ready!*, and then following the instructions to import a course into your new account, as covered in *Chapter 1, Getting Started with Canvas*.

Now that we have covered the **Canvas Guides** and the **Community Forums**, how to report a problem, and how to obtain pricing information for your institution, let's take a look at the last option on the Help menu: **Request a Feature**.

Requesting a feature

In your use of Canvas, you might come up with an idea for a feature that Canvas does not yet offer. As Canvas is an ever-evolving and constantly improving system that adapts its technology to the needs of the educators who use it, Canvas takes your suggestions very seriously. Before requesting a feature, double-check the **Canvas Guides** and the **Community Forums** to make sure the feature does not already exist. If you confirm that your idea hasn't yet been implemented, go ahead and request a new feature.

To request a feature, complete the following steps:

1. Open the **Help** menu by clicking on the link in the top-right or bottom menus, and then select the **Request a Feature** option, as pictured in the following screenshot:

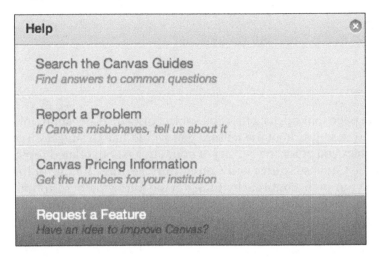

2. A new tab or window will open in your browser and you will see the **Community Forums** page for new feature suggestions. As mentioned previously, make sure that you search the forums for your suggestion before adding a new suggestion. If your idea is not already listed or available, click on the heading at the top-left section of the list of forums, which reads **After Searching, Start a New Discussion**, as shown in the following screenshot:

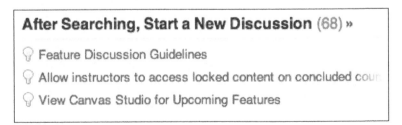

3. On the page that opens, you will see the first discussion listed as **Feature Discussion Guidelines**. Before submitting your request, go ahead and read this discussion for specific tips on how to suggest a feature and what you can do to increase the likelihood that your feature will be implemented in the future.

4. Once you have read this discussion, return to the main page and click on the **Request a Feature** button on the right-hand side, above the list of existing discussions, as shown in the following screenshot:

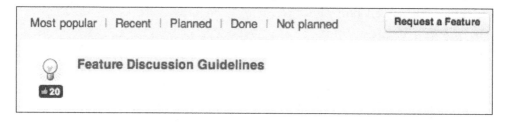

5. On the page that opens, enter the subject of your suggestion, followed by a detailed description of the feature you would like to suggest. You will notice that when you enter the subject of your suggestion, related topics will appear from the **Canvas Guides** and **Community Forums**. If none of the suggestions match your own, continue by filling in the following description. As with the other text boxes you have used within the Canvas Help Center, you can adjust the formatting using the menu below the main textbox and you can attach a file using the **Attach file** link in the bottom-left corner, as shown in the following screenshot:

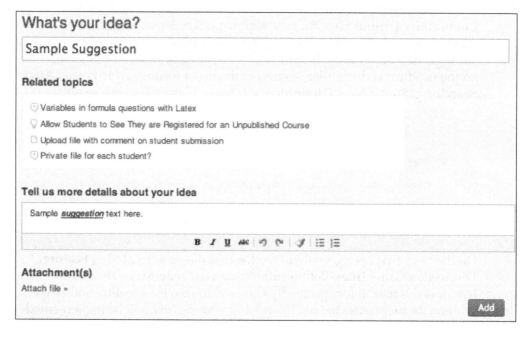

6. When you have entered all of the details of your suggestion, click on the **Add** button in the bottom-right corner.

After you have submitted your suggestion, other users will be able to see your request and personnel from Canvas will file it into the appropriate category on the **Feature Discussions Categories** page. Should your suggestion be chosen for implementation, you will most likely receive feedback from a Canvas employee and a **Planned** icon will appear next to the title of your discussion wherever it appears, as pictured in the following screenshot:

Make Import Assignment Group Optional   **Planned**
December 03, 2013 • Latest comment about 7 months ago • 💬 2

While your suggestions are very valuable and many user suggestions are later implemented, not all suggested features will be chosen for implementation. Your suggestion might be set aside for later discussion and can be brought back to the forefront if a large number of users express interest in seeing your suggestion implemented.

At this point, we have been through each of the options that are available to you should you need help with Canvas at any point. Before moving on and addressing alternative options to obtain help outside of Canvas, let's close this section with a list of important contact information should you need to get in touch with a Canvas employee to help solve your Canvas problems or answer your Canvas questions:

- Canvas Phone Numbers:
    - 1 (866) 494-1971 for information regarding Canvas
    - 1 (800) 203-6755 for general assistance with Canvas
- Canvas Information E-mail Address:
    - info@instructure.com
- Canvas Address:
    - 633 South 300 East, Suite 700, Salt Lake City, UT 84121

Let's now discuss alternative help options from outside of Canvas that you might choose to utilize if the problems or questions you encounter cannot be resolved using the built-in help options.

Finding help outside Canvas

Should you encounter a problem or question that is not addressed in the built-in help features of Canvas, the best option to consider is contacting your institution's **Information Technologies** (IT) department. Questions or problems that you might choose to direct to your institution's IT department, rather than Canvas directly, might include issues related to an institution-specific Internet server or information that is automatically imported, such as student rosters, course content, calendar events, external applications, or grading tools. There are a number of places where you might find the contact information for your institution's IT department, including the following:

- Your institution's phone or e-mail directory
- Your institution's website
- Fellow faculty or staff members

Related to the last bullet point, you can also reach out to fellow faculty members, staff, or students to ask for help with Canvas. If your institution has recently adopted Canvas as its LMS, chances are that other members of your school community have encountered similar problems or questions and might be able to help you find the answers to your questions.

Summary

In this chapter, we discussed how to find help within Canvas. We discussed how to access the **Help** menu through the link in the top-right or bottom menus. Then, we worked our way through each item on the **Help** menu. We discussed how to search the **Canvas Guides** and the **Community Forums** to see whether other Canvas users have already posed and answered your questions. Next, we walked through how to report a problem with Canvas. After that, we explored how to obtain Canvas pricing information as well as how to request a feature that you would like to see available through Canvas. After reviewing some of the contact information for Canvas that you might find useful when looking for an answer to your questions, we closed the chapter with a discussion of other places that you might be able to find help outside the Canvas website.

In our next and final chapter, you will learn how to export your course content for backup and transferring purposes, and we will also explore the ways in which Canvas can connect to the trends and requirements of education in the twenty-first century.

7
Now You're Ready!

As we begin our final chapter, let's take some time to learn how to export your course. We have explored a wide range of topics, focusing on learning what features Canvas offers, how to use those features, and the various options you have in customizing your Canvas course. As you finish teaching your course, you will be well served to export your course to keep as a backup, to upload and reteach later within Canvas to a new group of students, or to import into another LMS. After covering how to export your course, we will tie everything we've learned together through a discussion of how Canvas can help you and your students achieve educational goals while acquiring important 21st century skills. Overall, we will cover the following topics:

- Exporting your course from Canvas to your computer
- Connecting Canvas to education in the 21st century

Exporting your course

Now that your course is complete, you will want to export the course from Canvas to your computer. When you export your course, Canvas compiles all the information from your course and allows you to download a single file to your computer. This file will contain all of the information for your course, and you can use this file as a master template for each time you or your colleagues teach the course. Exporting your course is helpful for two main reasons:

- It is wise to save a back-up version of your course on a computer. After all the hard work you have put into building and teaching your course, it is always a good decision to export your course and save it to a computer. If you are using a Free for Teachers account, your course will remain intact and accessible online until you choose to delete it. However, if you use Canvas through your institution, each institution has different procedures and policies in place regarding what happens to courses when they are complete. Exporting and saving your course will preserve your hard work and protect it from any accidental or unintended deletion.

- Once you have exported your course, you will be able to import your course into Canvas at any point in the future. You are also able to import your course into other LMSs such as Moodle or BlackBoard. You might wish to import your course back into Canvas if your course is removed from your institution-specific Canvas account upon completion. You will have a copy of the course to import for the next time you are scheduled to teach the same course. You might build and teach a course using a Free for Teachers account, and then later wish to import that version of the course into an institution-specific Canvas account or another LMS.

Exporting your course does not remove the course from Canvas — your course will still be accessible on the Canvas site unless it is automatically deleted by your institution or if you choose to delete it.

 Exporting your course will only export the content of your course, not your students' assignment submissions or grades. Make sure that you download the grades for your course as well as students' individual assignment submissions if you wish to keep that information. To review how to download the grades or assignment submissions for your course, turn back to *Chapter 4, Teaching Your Canvas Course*.

To export your entire course, complete the following steps:

1. Click on the **Settings** tab at the bottom of the left-hand side menu, as pictured in the following screenshot:

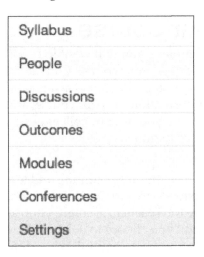

2. On the **Settings** page, look to the right-hand side menu. Click on the **Export Course Content** button, which is highlighted in the following screenshot:

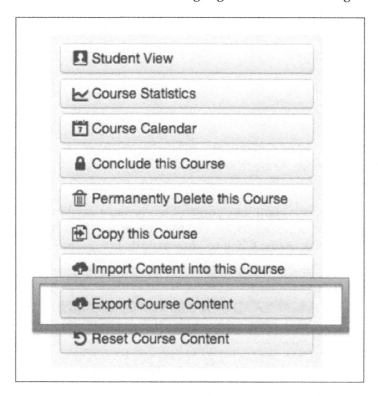

3. A screen will appear asking you whether you would like to export the **Course** or export a **Quiz**. To export your entire course, select the **Course** option and then click on **Create Export**, as shown in the following screenshot:

4. Once you click on **Create Export**, a progress bar will appear. As indicated in the message below the progress bar, the export might take a while to complete, and you can leave the page while Canvas exports the content. The following screenshot displays this progress bar and message:

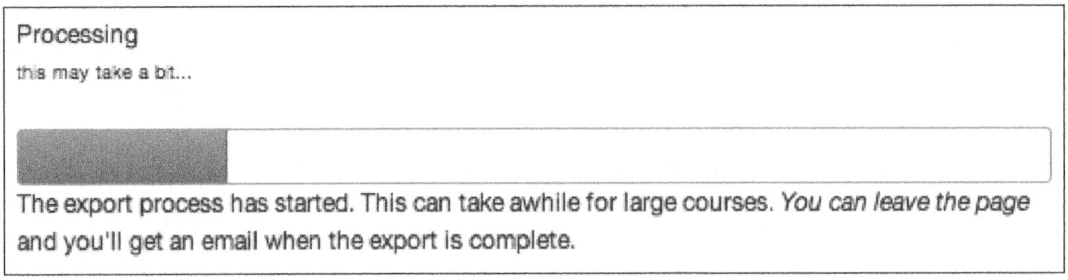

Processing

this may take a bit...

The export process has started. This can take awhile for large courses. *You can leave the page* and you'll get an email when the export is complete.

5. When the export is complete, you will receive an e-mail from notifications@instructure.com that resembles the following screenshot. Click on the **Click to view exports** link in the e-mail:

Your course export for *Canvas LMS Course Design* has finished.

Click to view exports

6. A new window or tab will appear in your browser that shows your **Content Exports**. Below the heading of the page, you will see your course export listed with a link that reads **Click here to download**, as pictured in the following screenshot. Go ahead and click on the link, and the course export file will be downloaded to your computer.

Content Exports

Course Export from Jan 3, 2014 3:12pm: Click here to download

7. Your course export file will be downloaded to your computer as a single .imscc file. You can then move the downloaded file to a folder on your computer's hard drive for later access.

Your course export is complete, and you can save the exported file for later use. To access the content stored in the exported `.imscc` file, you will need to import the file back into Canvas or another LMS. To review how to import a course, turn back to *Chapter 1*, *Getting Started with Canvas*.

 Your course export will include any announcements you have posted during the duration of your course, so you will most likely want to delete these announcements if you will be importing the course to use in a future class.

You might notice an option to **Conclude this Course** on the course **Settings** page if your institution has not hidden or disabled this option. In most cases, it is not necessary to conclude your course if you have set the correct course start and end dates in your **Course Details**. Concluding your course prevents you from altering grades or accessing course content, and you cannot *unconclude* your course on your own. Some institutions conclude courses automatically, which is why it is always best to export your course to preserve your work.

Now that we have covered the last how-to aspects of Canvas, let's close with some ways to apply the skills we have learned in this book to contemporary educational practices, philosophies, and requirements that you might encounter in your teaching.

Connecting Canvas to education in the 21st century

While learning how to use the features of Canvas, it is easy to forget the main purpose of Canvas' existence—to better serve your students and you in the process of education. In the midst of rapidly evolving technology, students and teachers alike require skills that are as adaptable and fluid as the technologies and new ideas swirling around them. While the development of various technologies might seem daunting, those involved in education in the 21st century have access to new and exciting tools that have never before existed. As an educator seeking to refine your craft, utilizing tools such as Canvas can help you and your students develop the skills that are becoming increasingly necessary to live and thrive in the 21st century. As attainment of these skills is indeed proving more and more valuable in recent years, many educational systems have begun to require evidence that instructors are cognizant of these skills and actively working to ensure that students are reaching valuable goals. The final sections of this book will offer some connections and examples of assignments that can help you utilize Canvas to meet the expectations of teaching in the 21st century.

Enacting the Framework for 21st Century Learning

As education across the world continues to evolve through time, the development of frameworks, methods, and philosophies of teaching have shaped the world of formal education. In recent years, one such approach that has gained prominence in the United States' education systems is the **Framework for 21st Century Learning**, which was developed over the last decade through the work of the **Partnership for 21st Century Skills (P21)**. This partnership between education, business, community, and government leaders was founded to help educators provide children in **Kindergarten through 12th Grade (K-12)** with the skills they would need going forward into the 21st century. Though the focus of P21 is on children in grades K-12, the concepts and knowledge articulated in the Framework for 21st Century Learning are valuable for learners at all levels, including those in higher education. In the following sections, we will apply our knowledge of Canvas to the desired 21st century student outcomes, as articulated in the P21 Framework for 21st Century Learning, to brainstorm the ways in which Canvas can help prepare your students for the future.

In the following sections, all information and quotations regarding the P21 Framework for 21st Century Learning come from the P21 Framework Definitions document, which is available at http://www.p21.org/storage/documents/ P21_Framework_Definitions.pdf.

Feel free to visit http://www.p21.org to learn more about the Partnership for 21st Century Skills and the valuable contributions they are making to contemporary education.

Core subjects and 21st century themes

The Framework for 21st Century Learning describes the importance of learning certain core subjects including English, reading or language arts, world languages, the arts, Mathematics, Economics, Science, Geography, History, Government, and Civics. In connecting these core subjects to the use of Canvas, the features of Canvas and the tips throughout this book should enable you to successfully teach courses in any of these subjects. In tandem with teaching and learning within the core subjects, P21 also advocates for schools to "promote understanding of academic content at much higher levels by weaving 21st century interdisciplinary themes into core subjects."

The following examples offer insight and ideas for ways in which Canvas can help you integrate these interdisciplinary themes into your course. As you read through the following suggestions and ideas, think about strategies that you might be able to implement into your existing curriculum to enhance its effectiveness and help your students engage with the P21 skills:

- **Global awareness**: Since it is accessible from anywhere with an Internet connection, Canvas opens the opportunity for a myriad of interactions across the globe. Utilizing Canvas as the platform for a purely online course enables students from around the world to enroll in your course. As a distance-learning tool in colleges, universities, or continuing education departments, Canvas has the capacity to unite students from anywhere in the world to directly interact with one another:

  - You might utilize the graded discussion feature for students to post a reflection about a class reading that considers their personal cultural background and how that affects their perception of the content. Taking it a step further, you might require students to *post a reply* comment on other students' reflections to further spark discussion, collaboration, and cross-cultural connections. As a reminder, it is always best to include an overview of online discussion etiquette somewhere within your course—you might consider adding a "Netiquette" section to your syllabus to maintain focus and a professional tone within these discussions.

  - You might set up a conference through Canvas with an international colleague as a guest lecturer for a course in any subject. As a prerequisite assignment, you might ask students to prepare three questions to ask the guest lecturer to facilitate a real-time international discussion within your class.

- **Financial, economic, business, and entrepreneurial literacy**: As the world becomes increasingly digitized, accessing and incorporating current content from the Web is a great way to incorporate financial, economic, business, and entrepreneurial literacy into your course:

  - In a Math course, you might consider creating a course module centered around the stock market. Within the module, you could build custom content pages offering direct instruction and introductions to specific topics. You could upload course readings and embed videos of interviews with experts with the YouTube app. You could link to live steam websites of the movement of the markets and create quizzes to assess students' understanding.

- **Civic literacy**: In fostering students' understanding of their role within their communities, Canvas can serve as a conduit of information regarding civic responsibilities, procedures, and actions:

    ° You might create a discussion assignment in which students search the Internet for a news article about a current event and post a reflection with connections to other content covered in the course. Offering guidance in your instructions to address how local and national citizenship impacts students' engagement with the event or incident could deepen the nature of responses you receive. Since discussion posts are visible to all participants in your course, a follow-up assignment might be for students to read one of the articles posted by another student and critique or respond to their reflection.

- **Health literacy:** Canvas can allow you to facilitate the exploration of health and wellness through the wide array of submission options for assignments. By utilizing the variety of assignment types you can create within Canvas, students are able to explore course content in new and meaningful ways:

    ° In a studio art class, you can create an out-of-class assignment to be submitted to Canvas in which students research the history, nature, and benefits of art therapy online and then create and upload a video sharing their personal relationship with art and connecting it to what they have found in the art therapy stories of others.

- **Environmental literacy**: As a cloud-based LMS, Canvas allows you to share files and course content with your students while maintaining and fostering an awareness of environmental sustainability:

    ° In any course you teach that involves readings uploaded to Canvas, encourage your students to download the readings to their computers or mobile devices rather than printing the content onto paper. Downloading documents to read on a device instead of printing them saves paper, reduces waste, and helps foster sustainable environmental habits. For PDF files embedded into content pages on Canvas, students can click on the preview icon that appears next to the document link and read the file directly on the content page without downloading or printing anything. Make a conscious effort to mention or address the environmental impacts of online learning versus traditional classroom settings, perhaps during a synchronous class conference or on a discussion board.

Learning and innovation skills

A number of specific elements combined can enable students to develop learning and innovation skills to prepare them for the increasingly "complex life and work environments in the 21st century." The communication setup of Canvas allows for quick and direct interactions while offering students the opportunity to contemplate and revise their contributions before posting to the course, submitting an assignment, or interacting with other students. This flexibility, combined with the ways in which you design your assignments, can help incorporate the following elements into your course to ensure the development of learning and innovation skills:

- **Creativity and innovation:** There are many ways in which the features of Canvas can help your students develop their creativity and innovation. As you build your course, finding ways for students to think creatively, work creatively with others, and implement innovations can guide the creation of your course assignments:

    - You might consider assigning groups of students to assemble a content page within Canvas dedicated to a chosen or assigned topic. Do so by creating a content page, and then enable any user within the course to edit the page. Allowing students to experiment with the capabilities of the Rich Content Editor, embedding outside content and synthesizing ideas within Canvas allows each group's creativity to shine.

    - As a follow-up assignment, you might choose to have students transfer the content of their content page to a public website or blog using sites such as Wikispaces, Wix, or Weebly. Once the sites are created, students can post their group site to a Canvas discussion page, where other students can view and interact with the work of their peers. Asking students to disseminate the class sites to friends or family around the globe could create international connections stemming from the creativity and innovation of your students' web content.

- **Critical thinking and problem solving**: As your students learn to overcome obstacles and find multiple solutions to complex problems, Canvas offers a place for students to work together to develop their critical thinking and problem-solving skills:

    - Assign pairs of students to debate and posit solutions to a global issue that connects to topics within your course. Ask students to use the **Conversations** feature of Canvas to debate the issue privately, finding supporting evidence in various forms from around the Internet. Using the **Collaborations** feature, ask each pair of students to assemble and submit a final e-report on the topic, presenting the various solutions they came up with as well as supporting evidence in various electronic forms such as articles, videos, news clips, and websites.

- **Communication and collaboration**: With the seemingly impersonal nature of electronic communication, communication skills are incredibly important to maintain intended meanings across multiple means of communication. As the nature of online collaboration and communication poses challenges for understanding, connotation, and meaning, honing communication skills becomes increasingly important:

    ° As a follow-up assignment to the preceding debate suggestion, use the conferences tool in Canvas to set up a full class debate. During the debate, ask each pair of students to present their final e-report to the class, followed by a group discussion of each pair's findings, solutions, and conclusions. You might find it useful for each pair to explain their process and describe the challenges and/or benefits of collaborating and communicating via the Internet in contrast to collaborating and communicating in person.

Information, media, and technology skills

The rapid growth of electronic technology and the ubiquitous influence of the Internet on life in the 21st century has not gone unnoticed in the realm of education. Many administrators expect teachers of all levels to stay up-to-date on the most current technologies and trends that can increase student engagement, and thus, student achievement. As shown in the following examples, ways to exercise information, media, and technology skills for your students are abundant when using Canvas:

- **Information literacy:** The ease with which anyone in the entire world can post and circulate information on the Internet is greater than ever before. As such, students need to be able to judge the quality, accuracy, and validity of the information they encounter:

    ° Set up a discussion assignment in which students are required to post an article related to an assigned topic. Before posting the article they find, students must check other students' posts to make sure no one else has posted the same article. Once all of the different articles are posted, require students to pick two articles posted by other students. For each chosen article, ask students to post a critique of the quality, accuracy, and validity of each article and its source.

- **Media literacy**: Information can be confounded as it passes through various forms of media before reaching the general public. Canvas Apps connect to a variety of media outlets and sources, so utilizing Canvas Apps to compare and contrast information via various forms of media can refine your students' perception:

    ° Enable the Wikipedia, New York Times, and USA Today apps for your course. Create an assignment, and then within the description for that assignment, search for and embed articles that present information on the same topic or event from Wikipedia, the New York Times, and USA Today. Following these embedded articles, instruct students to compare and contrast the information from each media outlet and submit a written, video, or audio response sharing their findings.

- **Information, Communications, and Technology (ICT) literacy**: The mere act of using Canvas immediately begins to hone students' ICT literacy, as using Canvas requires the development and use of basic ICT skills. By using Canvas, students are processing information from a variety of sources, building an understanding of modern communication and exercising their knowledge of computers and mobile devices to execute complex tasks:

    ° At the beginning of any course you teach, ask students to pay close attention to all of the steps required to access, configure, and begin using Canvas. Once all of the students are successfully enrolled in your course, ask them to reflect on all of the skills they used to begin using Canvas. You might choose to create a discussion or an assignment where students can submit their reflections, and you can give students the option to submit their reflections in a written, video, or audio format (each of which requires varied and unique ICT skills).

Life and career skills

It seems that in the whirlwind of education, teachers try frantically to cover as much content as possible while other imperative life skills are thrown to the wayside. In working to educate your students, keeping in mind the goal of helping them develop as well-rounded, whole individuals is incredibly important. Not only are life and career skills important for students' individual happiness and well-being, these skills are invaluable as your students seek to build relationships, achieve personal goals, and realize a desirable, fulfilling future. Keeping in mind the seemingly impersonal nature of online communication, it is important to consciously integrate these skills into the courses you create using Canvas. Fortunately, the array of features within Canvas makes this an attainable goal that can often develop organically as you design and create assignments:

- **Flexibility and adaptability**: As mentioned earlier, students and teachers in the 21st century need skills that are as flexible and adaptable as the ever-changing technology around them. Canvas frequently updates and adds to the current features, so simply using Canvas over an extended period of time can help both students and teachers learn to be flexible and adapt to new situations:

    ○ Within the time constraints of your course, there are bound to be some necessary adjustments. Using the course calendar and the conversations tools, communicating changes and adaptations within your course can help students become flexible learners. Explicitly mentioning the value of being able to adapt can help students conceptualize these skills in a more concrete way. Canvas also offers some built-in notification features that help students prepare for adjustments, such as the **Notify users that this content has changed** checkbox (pictured in the following screenshot) when editing an assignment. Checking this box makes it easy to let users know when you have updated or altered the expectations for an assignment, which requires flexibility and adaptability on the part of the student:

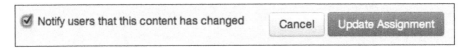

- **Initiative and self-direction**: In today's school and work environments, learning to be a self-guided learner who takes the initiative to gain knowledge and solve problems is an incredibly valuable skill. The expanse of the World Wide Web is at your disposal as an instructor using Canvas, and helping your students realize that that expanse is also open to them can help guide them to take the initiative and direct their own learning:

    ° Create an assignment that purposely forces your students to take a leap into the unknown. You might choose to introduce a challenging new topic that they have not encountered before, pose a question or problem that requires knowledge not yet covered in the course, or utilize an external tool that requires procedural skills only found elsewhere online. Carefully explain that you expect students to search the Web to find the information they need to complete the assignment, and that their success with the assignment depends on the quality and content of the resources they find. While education typically follows a scaffolded approach where new knowledge builds on previous knowledge, an occasional foray into the unknown is an excellent exercise to develop students' initiative and self-direction.

    ° Encourage students to explore the huge array of open online courses at http://www.canvas.net, which hosts Canvas' **Massive Open Online Course (MOOC)** options that are free and open for anyone around the world to take. Like other MOOCs available online, the open courses on the **Canvas Network** allow students to explore topics of interest on their own by enrolling in other online courses free of charge.

- **Social and cross-cultural skills:** Fostering empathy and understanding between your students often pervades the beginning of any class you teach. Setting the tone of your course from the very beginning is incredibly important to help your students learn in a comfortable, safe, and supportive environment. Teachers in traditional classroom settings often cover these expectations during the first few classes, and you can cover these same ideas within your Canvas course as well:

    ° Within your course syllabus description, the home page description of your course, or each assignment description, clearly communicate the social and cross-cultural skills you expect to see your students display during the course. Reminding students to consider how others in the class might perceive their comments on discussion boards, during conferences, or within private messages can help develop the skills and frame of mind necessary to flourish in a social environment. As mentioned previously, consider adding a *Netiquette* section to your syllabus to articulate the positive, productive online communication skills you expect to see students utilize during your course.

- **Productivity and accountability**: Traditional live classes often meet many times a week, and as your students attend each class, they are reminded of the work they are expected to complete for each meeting. Courses within Canvas that do not have a live component force students to manage their time independently as they complete their work outside of a traditional classroom setting. Students are expected to complete and submit their work in a timely fashion without the reminders they receive by attending a live class multiple times a week:

  ○ While it is always a good idea to post announcements and send out reminders in conversations a day or two before assignments are due in the beginning of your course, let students know that as your course progresses, they will be responsible for managing their own productivity and you will hold them accountable for their performance throughout the course. Keep in mind the age group with which you are working, and maintain realistic, age-appropriate expectations throughout your course. When students are first learning how to use Canvas and getting used to your expectations within the online learning platform, you might consider some leniency with late submissions, but coupled with feedback communicating your expectations for timely submissions in the future. It is important to help your students succeed, but it is valuable to get students on the right track initially and then let them monitor themselves for the rest of your time together. The communication features of Canvas allow you to do this on an individual basis or for the entire group, so take advantage of these features to ensure your students' success.

- **Leadership and responsibility**: When designing your assignments and activities, it is important to find ways for your students to hone their leadership skills and to demonstrate responsibility within Canvas. Think of ways to explore the individual and community aspects of your course to help students develop these valuable skills:

° Organize participants in your course into user groups or create group assignments. Over the course of multiple group assignments or group activities, ask one student from each group to be the "group leader". Using the conversation and collaborations features of Canvas, have the groups work together to accomplish the assignment or activity. Set up a discussion board or conference where each group leader presents the work for the entire group. Over the duration of your course, make sure that each student in the class serves as the group leader at least once. You might also consider creating a follow-up assignment for the group leader in which each student reflects on the specific challenges and successes they encountered while being the group leader. The directions for the reflection might ask students to discuss how their experience as the group leader contributed to their leadership skills and sense of personal or group responsibility.

The Framework for 21st Century Learning offers a wide array of concepts, skills, and attributes that are valuable for students to attain during the course of their education. The suggested activities in the preceding section offer just a small sample of ideas that you might be able to implement within your courses to help your students develop these important skills. As you work to help your students excel in the content area of your course and develop useful life skills, consider how modeling behavior in a live classroom can be one of the most powerful tools in a teacher's set of resources. Transfer this idea to teaching with Canvas; as you strive to master the technology of Canvas and as you interact with your students, think about how you are demonstrating and modeling the skills you would like to see in your students. Consider how your electronic communication reflects on your overall communication skills; do you seem like a different person online than you do in person? How does your leadership style relate to the traits you would like to see develop in your students? Do your assignments reflect the creative and unique nature of the responses you hope to receive from your students? The list goes on and on, so as you continue to improve your teaching, try to demonstrate the attitudes and behaviors you would want your students to exhibit in class, whether that class is a fully live class, a hybrid live course with online expectations, or a fully online experience.

Summary

In this chapter, we brought our work to a close. We began with the final step-by-step element of this book as we learned how to export your course. Next, we worked to apply the technical knowledge we have gained to practical educational resources that you are likely to encounter as an educator. We covered each of the four 21st Century Student Outcomes as articulated in the P21 Framework for 21st Century Learning in detail, discussing the importance of each outcome and offering concrete examples of ways you might use Canvas to help students achieve these outcomes.

At the close of this book, it is important to keep in mind the reason that Canvas exists: education. Everything we have discussed in the last seven chapters should help you in your quest to becoming a better, more effective teacher. Through Canvas, you can help your students engage with course content and help empower them to take ownership of their learning. It is important to remember that Canvas is an educational tool, and you have the opportunity and responsibility to use it to better the quality of your students' lives. With the skills you have gained, you can now work to create exciting, engaging, and unique learning experiences for you and your students using Canvas.

The final chapter, *Appendix, References and Resources*, will provide you with a number of valuable resources that you might find helpful in your current and future work with Canvas, online course design, general online learning, and practical applications of educational philosophy.

References and Resources

The following sections offer information on materials referenced throughout this book and other resources that you might find helpful as you learn and grow as an online educator. While many of these resources do not mention Canvas specifically, they reference broader topics related to teaching and learning in the 21st century, designing online learning environments, and conceptualizing online education. The description of each resource in the following sections includes connections to Canvas that you might find helpful as you explore online education through Canvas.

> As a reminder, you can always find help with Canvas within the Canvas Guides and Community Forums, as discussed in *Chapter 6, Where to Go for Help*. You can find these resources at http://guides.canvas.com should you need assistance with Canvas directly.

Teaching and learning in the 21st century

As discussed in *Chapter 7, Now You're Ready!*, Canvas offers a wide array of features that allow you to address contemporary trends in education. The resources and books described in the following sections will provide you with more specific information about current best practices in teaching and learning.

Partnership for 21st Century Skills

- **Authors**: Partnership between educational leaders from 19 states in the US and 26 organizations.
- **Website**: http://www.p21.org.

- **Description**: Partnership for 21st Century Skills (P21) provides valuable information regarding skills gleaned from educational experiences that will enhance the lives of learners in the 21st century. These skills go beyond traditional behaviorist goals to include more complex thought processes by making connections, synthesizing information, and thinking critically. The P21 Framework for 21st Century Learning has been adopted as a contemporary best practice in education throughout the United States with worldwide implications. The details of the P21 skills and framework are freely available online at the P21 website.

- **Connections to Canvas**: *Chapter 7, Now You're Ready!*, includes a detailed discussion of the ways in which Canvas can help you connect to and address a wide variety of 21st century skills in a live, online, or hybrid course. Familiarizing yourself with these skills can inform you about the ways in which you might choose to utilize Canvas to enhance your students' learning experience.

- **Further Reading**: A number of publications address the P21 skills and framework, including *21st Century Skills: Learning for Life in Our Times* by Bernie Trilling and Charles Fadel, published by Jossey-Bass.

Understanding by Design

- **Authors**: Grant Wiggins and Jay McTighe
- **ISBN**: 978-0131950849
- **Publisher**: Pearson (Expanded 2nd Edition)
- **Description**: *Understanding by Design* presents ways to conceptualize curriculum design to ensure lasting student understanding. Addressing the contemporary push for standards-based education, components of Understanding by Design such as Backwards Design, the Six Facets of Understanding, Essential Questions, and Teaching for Understanding offer ways to ensure that your students are able to fully understand and utilize content to meet the educational standards of your country, district, or institution. A number of resources related to Understanding by Design are available online for free in addition to a wide range of publications available for purchase in printed format.

- **Connections to Canvas**: As you work to design your Canvas courses, referring to the concepts and techniques articulated in the Understanding by Design literature can help you ensure that your course design, assessments, and outcomes are all aligned with one another to ensure maximum student understanding and retention of information. The Outcomes feature of Canvas offers you a unique way to directly incorporate the standards of your country, district, or institution into your course, and incorporating strategies of Understanding by Design can further aid you in helping your students attain these outcomes.

Creating Significant Learning Experiences: An Integrated Approach to Designing College Courses

- **Author:** L. Dee Fink
- **ISBN:** 978-1118124253
- **Publisher:** Jossey-Bass (Revised and Updated)
- **Website:** http://www.deefinkandassociates.com
- **Description:** Considering the tremendous changes, developments, and advances within higher education in recent decades, this book offers you insight into new research on learning in higher education as well as research regarding Fink's popular instructional design model used in colleges and universities around the world. This revised edition presents examples of Fink's model from online education, explores how student engagement impacts student learning, and suggests strategies for addressing resistance from students to innovative teaching strategies within higher education.
- **Connections to Canvas:** Though the trend of online learning has begun to spread to institutions serving students of younger ages, online learning started and has remained prominent within higher education. Fink's instructional design model offers guidance for instructors of college-aged learners and integrates current research to support best practices in instructional design. This book can offer context, guidance, and scholarly grounding for you as you work to build and teach your Canvas course within a higher education environment.

Designing online learning environments

In the following section, you will find a number of resources that offer specific strategies for designing and developing cooperative, productive, and meaningful online learning communities in which you and your students can engage with one another as well as the content of your course. These resources include general strategies that might be implemented across any number of LMSs, or they might include techniques specific to one LMS. By comparing the ways in which you might use Canvas to strategies that other educators have used with alternate LMSs, you can expand your understanding of the possibilities of online learning and find unique ways to enhance your Canvas courses.

How to Design and Teach a Hybrid Course: Achieving Student-Centered Learning through Blended Classroom, Online and Experiential Activities

- **Author:** Jay Caulfield
- **ISBN:** 978-1579224233
- **Publisher:** Stylus Publishing
- **Description:** Exploring the educational philosophy and theories behind hybrid courses as well as the actual design and implementation of such courses, this book explores the ways in which combining live and online components in a course can impact student achievement and understanding. Hybrid courses allow instructors and students to take advantage of the best aspects of traditional and online learning environments, and this book offers you techniques to ensure a meaningful educational experience for all involved.
- **Connections to Canvas:** Hybrid courses have been a topic of discussion throughout this book, and many of the chapters have addressed ways in which you can utilize Canvas within a hybrid teaching situation. You can directly implement the concepts covered in *How to Design and Teach a Hybrid Course: Achieving Student-Centered Learning through Blended Classroom, Online and Experiential Activities* into your Canvas course in order to foster collaboration, student-guided learning, and ownership of material through both contemporary and traditional best practices.

Discussion-Based Online Teaching To Enhance Student Learning: Theory, Practice and Assessment

- **Author:** Tisha Bender
- **ISBN 13:** 978-1579227470
- **Publisher:** Stylus Publishing

- **Description:** Discussion-based activities are a powerful means of engaging online learners and creating opportunities for interacting with content in meaningful ways. This book looks into the distinction between "digital natives", the generation of students and teachers who have grown up surrounded by technology, and "digital immigrants", the generation of teachers and students during whose lifetime current technologies have developed. Included in this resource are a myriad of ways in which teachers might be able to design online course activities to more effectively encourage cooperation through discussion-based collaboration.

- **Connections to Canvas:** Canvas offers you numerous outlets for collaboration and cooperation through discussion-based activities such as the Discussions, Collaborations, Conversations, and Conferences features. Applying the philosophical considerations and instructional strategies within this resource to your Canvas course can increase the quality and sophistication of discussion-based elements in your course.

The Gamification of Learning and Instruction: Game-based Methods and Strategies for Training and Education

- **Author:** Karl M. Kapp
- **ISBN:** 978-1118096345
- **Publisher:** John Wiley & Sons
- **Description:** This book offers an exciting look into the process of Gamification, or reframing learning through the lens of a game. As a means of increasing engagement with content, designing learning experiences as games offers the potential to help students apply and retain the knowledge they gain as they work through information embedded in various game concepts.

- **Connections to Canvas:** The layout options and customizable features of Canvas make it an excellent platform for gamified learning. Within sequential modules that only unlock once students complete certain activities, you can build custom content pages full of embedded content and incorporate them into outside resources that could function as levels or worlds of a game. As we have focused so much on the importance of sequence, structure, and scaffolding in choosing your course design, considering a gamified version of your course could offer your students unique and lasting interactions with the content of your course.

Blackboard Essentials for Teachers

- **Author:** William Rice
- **ISBN:** 978-1849692922
- **Publisher:** Packt Publishing

- **Description:** Taking a look at the specifics of the Blackboard LMS, this book offers an in-depth insight into how to use the Blackboard system to design and teach courses. Exploring the full features offered through Blackboard, this book walks you through the steps of building and teaching a course.

- **Connections to Canvas:** Blackboard is another very popular LMS that many schools around the world use to host course content. Exploring the options available through other LMSs and seeing the types of content and activities demonstrated in *Blackboard Essentials for Teachers*, you can further your understanding of how you might adapt and improve your course design within Canvas. With the wide array of tools and features available through Canvas, exploring options available through other LMSs can offer you new ideas for your own courses.

- **Further Reading:** If you would like more insight into what the behind-the-scenes management of an LMS looks like for an institution, consider checking out *Blackboard Learn Administration*, which explores the administrative side of managing the Blackboard LMS:

  ○ **Author:** Terry Patterson
  ○ **ISBN:** 978-1849693066
  ○ **Publisher:** Packt Publishing

Conceptualizing online education

As time moves forward, advancements in education, technology, and culture pose challenges regarding relevancy for teachers and learners. We struggle with determining what information is the most valuable for the coming generations to know and finding the best means of sharing that information with those generations. Online and distance learning are relatively new concepts in the world of education, and finding a balance between traditional approaches and contemporary practices can be challenging. Many educators, authors, and policy makers have worked to address these challenges for teachers by illuminating the immense opportunities available through new technologies, philosophies, and strategies. Finding ways to conceptualize online learning within the historical context of education and the advancements of the modern era is vital to ensure relevant, meaningful education for our students. The following resources offer excellent ways to understand, frame, and reframe online learning within the context of traditional and contemporary education.

Building Online Learning Communities: Effective Strategies for the Virtual Classroom

- **Authors:** Rena M. Palloff and Keith Pratt
- **ISBN:** 978-0787988258

- **Publisher:** Jossey-Bass (Second Edition)

- **Description:** Offering many real-life examples from successful online courses, this book examines the ways in which instructors can foster a sense of community among students in an online environment. Considerations include the engagement of learners not only with content, but with one another, as well as how to encourage self-guided learning and motivation among students.

- **Connections to Canvas:** As online learning becomes increasingly ubiquitous in higher education, one of the chief fears and criticisms is the impersonal nature of early online learning platforms. Focusing on establishing a personal, "real" presence in your virtual classroom can be achieved through a number of features offered in Canvas such as announcements, discussions, conferences, and conversations. Finding ways to build a unified group of learners who can collaborate with and rely upon one another is sure to improve your students' achievement and overall success in your course.

Essentials of Online Course Design: A Standards-Based Guide

- **Authors:** Marjorie Val and Kristen Sosulski

- **ISBN:** 978-0415873000

- **Publisher:** Routledge

- **Website:** http://essentialsofonlinecoursedesign.blogspot.com

- **Description:** Presenting a methodical, standards-based approach for designing and building online courses, this book focuses on the pedagogical, organizational, and visual elements of course design that will ensure ease of use for both instructors and teachers. To help users avoid confusion and disengagement with content, following the steps in this guide will help instructors design courses that present information clearly and logically to promote maximum engagement and achievement.

- **Connections to Canvas:** Making sure your students feel comfortable and at ease with their online learning experience is key in helping them understand the content and obtain desired outcomes. With the flexibility and customizations inherent in Canvas as an LMS, you are able to present only the most pertinent, valuable information and features, while hiding unnecessary or confusing tools. You are able to control the left-hand side menu items that students see, and you can choose from a wide range of layout designs that make it clear and simple for your students to participate in the course. The ideas within *Essentials of Online Course Design: A Standards-Based Guide* can help you on your journey to creating an intuitive, clear, concise, and robust online learning experience.

Best Practices for Teaching with Emerging Technologies

- **Author:** Michelle Pacansky-Brock
- **Series:** Best Practices in Online Teaching and Learning
- **ISBN:** 978-0415899390
- **Publisher:** Routledge
- **Description:** With the vast array of social media and Internet resources at the disposal of educators utilizing online technologies, finding ways to integrate web-based tools into educational settings while maintaining student privacy is an important goal for contemporary educators. Exploring social media, web-based tools, and mobile device options, this book presents valuable tools at a variety of prices for educators teaching in live, hybrid, or online settings.
- **Connections to Canvas:** Connecting your Canvas account to your social media accounts, integrating apps into your Canvas course, and encouraging students to use the Canvas mobile app are just some of the ways in which you can connect to the students in your Canvas course. Considering the ideas and concepts included in *Best Practices for Teaching with Emerging Technologies* can further your understanding of ways in which you might connect with your students and help them integrate participation in your course into their digital lives.

Online Teaching and Learning Series Books

The Online Teaching and Learning (OTL) series from Jossey-Bass covers a tremendous range of topics regarding online learning experiences. Books in this series include step-by-step guides as well as explorations of topics including student engagement, assessment, collaboration, and inclusion.

The following books from the OTL series will prove valuable additions to your collection of resources, and each connects to topics directly covered in our exploration of Canvas as a platform for online course content:

- **Conquering the Content: A Step-by-Step Guide to Online Course Design**
   - **Author:** Robin M. Smith
   - **ISBN:** 978-0787994426

- **Engaging the Online Learner: Activities and Resources for Creative Instruction, Updated Edition**
   - **Authors:** Rita-Marie Conrad and J. Ana Donaldson
   - **ISBN:** 978-1118018194

- **Learning Online with Games, Simulations, and Virtual Worlds: Strategies for Online Instruction**
  - ° **Author:** Clark Aldrich
  - ° **ISBN:** 978-0470438343

- **Assessing the Online Learner: Resources and Strategies for Faculty**
  - ° **Authors:** Rena M. Palloff and Keith Pratt
  - ° **ISBN:** 978-0470283868

- **Using Wikis for Online Collaboration: The Power of the Read-Write Web**
  - ° **Authors:** James A. West and Margaret L. West
  - ° **ISBN:** 978-0470343333

- **Collaborating Online: Learning Together in Community**
  - ° **Authors:** Rena M. Palloff and Keith Pratt
  - ° **ISBN:** 978-0787976149

- **Making Online Teaching Accessible: Inclusive Course Design for Students with Disabilities**
  - ° **Author:** Norman Coombs
  - ° **ISBN:** 978-0470499047

Other online course design resources

In addition to the resources listed previously, there are many more resources available online that deal with designing online courses, ensuring the high quality of online learning opportunities, and utilizing best practices. The following list includes further resources that you may find helpful, but feel free to explore the Web for your own resources as you work to improve your approach to online education.

The Blended Learning Toolkit

- **Prepared by**: University of Central Florida (UCF) and American Association of State Colleges and Universities (AASCU)
- **Website**: http://blended.online.ucf.edu

The 5 Pillars – Sloan-C Quality Framework

- **Prepared by**: Online Learning Consortium (formerly the Sloan Consortium)
- **Website**: http://onlinelearningconsortium.org/5pillars

Quality Matters: A National Benchmark for Online Course Design

- **Prepared by**: MarylandOnline
- **Website**: http://www.qualitymatters.org

Quality Course Framework: A Framework for Developing Quality Course Environments

- **Prepared by**: The University of Utah
- **Website**: http://tlt.utah.edu/qcf/

Teaching Online: Design of an Online Course

- **Prepared by**: The University of Central Florida
- **Website**: http://teach.ucf.edu/pedagogy/design-of-an-online-course/

CanvasLMS YouTube Channel

- **Prepared by**: Instructure Canvas and YouTube
- **Website**: http:// www.youtube.com/user/CanvasLMS

Index

A

account settings
  adjusting 18
  cell phone number, adding for SMS text
      notifications 19, 20
  general settings, editing 20-23
  new e-mail address, adding 18
  notification preferences, customizing 24-27
  registered services, using 23, 24
announcements
  posting 115, 116
apps
  integrating, into course 166-168
Assessment
  rubrics, using for 164-166
assignment
  about 65
  adding 41
  creating 41, 42
  editing 43
  publishing 62, 63
  rubrics, adding to 162-164
  updating 62, 63
assignment availability 62
assignment groups
  creating 74, 75
  weighting 76
Assignment List layout 99, 100
assignment types
  Assignment 65
  creating 63, 64
  Discussion assignment 65-67
  external tools, enabling 74
  Not Graded assignment 74
  Quiz assignment 67, 68

B

basic formatting, Rich Content Editor 44
BlackBoard 202

C

Canvas
  Announcements feature 115
  connecting, to education in
      21st Century 205
  Conversations feature 107
  Help, finding within 175, 176
  URL 135, 213
  using, on mobile devices 133
Canvas accounts
  Free for Teachers Canvas accounts 8
  Institution-specific Canvas accounts 7
Canvas Community Forums
  exploring 177
  questions, asking in 182-185
  response, providing to questions in 185-187
Canvas dashboard
  navigating 11-13
Canvas Guides
  browsing 177-180
  exploring 177
  searching 180, 181
  URL 217
Canvas Guides menu
  Mobile Guides - Canvas by Instructure 179
  Mobile Guides - MagicMarker 179
  Mobile Guides - Polls for Canvas 179
  Mobile Guides - SpeedGrader 179
Canvas mobile app
  configuring 134-137

institution's Canvas site
  accessing 8, 9
  course, creating 28, 29
Institution-specific Canvas accounts 7
Instructure app 133

J

Jing
  about 190
  downloading 191
  used, for creating screencast 190-194

K

Khan Academy app 167
Kindergarten through 12th
        Grade (K-12) 206

L

learning management system (LMS) 7, 33
life and career skills, P21
  about 212
  accountability 214
  adaptability 212
  cross-cultural skills 213
  flexibility 212
  initiative 213
  leadership 214, 215
  productivity 214
  responsibility 214, 215
  self-direction 213
  social skills 213
Links tab 56
Link to URL feature 46

M

Massive Open Online Course (MOOC) 213
Media Recordings option 60
messages
  sending, within Canvas mobile app 140-143
  viewing, within Canvas mobile app 140-143
mobile devices
  Canvas, using on 133
Moodle 202

N

navigation links
  selecting 89-91
New York app 211
Not Graded assignment 74
notification preferences
  customizing 24-27
notifications
  accessing, within Canvas mobile app 144

O

online education
  design resources 225, 226
  resources, for conceptualizing 222-224
online learning environments
  designing 220-222
Outcome
  creating 152-155
  using 159-161
Outcome Groups
  creating 155-157

P

P21 Framework
  about 206
  URL 206
P21 Framework, for 21st Century Learning
  21st Century Themes 206
  about 206
  core subjects 206
  Information, Communications and
        Technology (ICT) literacy 211
  information literacy 210
  innovation skills 209, 210
  learning skills 209, 210
  life and career skills 212
  media literacy 210, 211
  URL 206
participants
  adding, to course 79-84
  user groups, creating 87-89
  users, managing 85-87
Partnership for 21st Century Skills. *See*
        P21 Framework
peer reviews 61

Thank you for buying
Canvas LMS Course Design

About Packt Publishing

Packt, pronounced 'packed', published its first book "*Mastering phpMyAdmin for Effective MySQL Management*" in April 2004 and subsequently continued to specialize in publishing highly focused books on specific technologies and solutions.

Our books and publications share the experiences of your fellow IT professionals in adapting and customizing today's systems, applications, and frameworks. Our solution based books give you the knowledge and power to customize the software and technologies you're using to get the job done. Packt books are more specific and less general than the IT books you have seen in the past. Our unique business model allows us to bring you more focused information, giving you more of what you need to know, and less of what you don't.

Packt is a modern, yet unique publishing company, which focuses on producing quality, cutting-edge books for communities of developers, administrators, and newbies alike. For more information, please visit our website: www.packtpub.com.

About Packt Open Source

In 2010, Packt launched two new brands, Packt Open Source and Packt Enterprise, in order to continue its focus on specialization. This book is part of the Packt Open Source brand, home to books published on software built around Open Source licenses, and offering information to anybody from advanced developers to budding web designers. The Open Source brand also runs Packt's Open Source Royalty Scheme, by which Packt gives a royalty to each Open Source project about whose software a book is sold.

Writing for Packt

We welcome all inquiries from people who are interested in authoring. Book proposals should be sent to author@packtpub.com. If your book idea is still at an early stage and you would like to discuss it first before writing a formal book proposal, contact us; one of our commissioning editors will get in touch with you.

We're not just looking for published authors; if you have strong technical skills but no writing experience, our experienced editors can help you develop a writing career, or simply get some additional reward for your expertise.

Desire2Learn for Higher Education Cookbook

ISBN: 978-1-84969-344-8   Paperback: 206 pages

Gain expert knowledge of the tools within the Desire2Learn Learning Environment, maximize your productivity, and create online learning experiences with these easy-to-follow recipes

1. Customize the look and feel of your online course, integrate graphics and video, and become more productive using the learning environment's built-in assessment and collaboration tools.

2. Recipes address real world challenges in clear and concise step-by-step instructions, which help you work your way through technical tasks with ease.

Blackboard Learn Administration

ISBN: 978-1-84969-306-6   Paperback: 326 pages

Discover how to administrate your Blackboard Learn platform through step-by-step tutorials

1. Learn both the simple and the complex skills to become an expert Blackboard Learn admin.

2. Optimize the security and performance of Blackboard Learn and create a disaster recovery plan.

3. Gain insight from an experienced Blackboard administrator using a hands-on approach.

Please check **www.PacktPub.com** for information on our titles

Moodle 2.5 Multimedia Cookbook
Second Edition

ISBN: 978-1-78328-937-0   Paperback: 300 pages

75 recipes to help you integrate different multimedia resources into your Moodle courses to make them more interactive

1. Add all sorts of multimedia features to your Moodle course.

2. Lots of easy-to-follow, step-by-step recipes.

3. Work with sound, audio, and animation to make your course even more interactive.

HTML5 Graphing and Data Visualization Cookbook

ISBN: 978-1-84969-370-7   Paperback: 344 pages

Learn how to create interactive HTML5 charts and graphs with canvas, JavaScript, and open source tools

1. Build interactive visualizations of data from scratch with integrated animations and events.

2. Draw with canvas and other HTML5 elements that improve your ability to draw directly in the browser.

3. Work and improve existing third-party charting solutions such as Google Maps.

Please check **www.PacktPub.com** for information on our titles

20134431R00139

Made in the USA
Middletown, DE
09 December 2018